What People Are Saying About
THE *TRANSITION* LEADER

The Transition Leader is a must-read for those who love the local church. Through his years of experience, Ron McManus shares thought-provoking insights, personal stories, and principles that foster healthy [leadership] transitions. I know these principles work; Ron transitioned the thriving church I now Pastor.

Mark English
Lead Pastor, Christian Life Church

God has used Dr. Ron McManus to help churches going through a transition with their Lead Pastor.

Before my installation as Lead Pastor of Grand Rapids First, Ron led the church for ten months as the Interim Lead Pastor. During that time, Ron's wisdom and guidance were critical in stabilizing and preparing the congregation, the church board, and the pastoral team for a successful transition.

In *The Transition Leader*, Ron shares principles from his 20-plus years of experience that will help any church walking through or anticipating a transition.

Sam Rijfkogel
Lead Pastor, Grand Rapids First

Ron McManus stepped into the role of interim pastor after our lead pastor of 33 years was elected to district office in 2019. We were 4 months into a worldwide pandemic. Ron's experience with transitioning churches was extremely critical during those days of uncertainty and fear. Navigating through the fog of Covid, Ron's presence was both reassuring behind the pulpit and in front of the staff. The word "maintain" is not in his vocabulary. He challenged us to get out into the community and demonstrate the love of God through acts of compassion, all the while working with our search committee behind the scenes walking through the process of finding our next lead pastor. God was faithful through it all and in due season at the right time, sent us the right person to lead us for years to come. We owe a debt of gratitude to Ron for his pastoral leadership through a season the likes of which I have never seen before.

Tom Blackwood
Executive Pastor

I know of no one else who has more first-hand and hand-on experience in assisting church in Pastoral transitions than my long-time friend Ron McManus. Ron loves the Church and Pastors. He has served as interim Pastor of many significant churches, nursed them to health and successfully transitioned to the church's next and permanent Pastor. This book is pure gold for those who want to sustain and scale His Church.

Sam Chand
A friend of Ron McManus

I can think of no one better equipped to help a leader or local church effectively engage the art of a church transition than my friend, Ron McManus. Through his many years of extraordinary experience, Ron has so much to offer to every type of transition, whether helping a long-time leader build a succession plan, coaching a soldier among the rising army of transitional pastors, or preparing a congregation to embrace their leader of the future. Ron has done it all, again and again, and with remarkable success. Given the large number of transitions already underway and the tidal wave of such challenges on the horizon, few books are as needed as this one. The futures of many congregations, large and small, and the great impact and hope many are bringing today to their needy communities, demand that we navigate the challenging waters of leadership transition with maximum wisdom—the kind that Ron McManus has packed into this vital leadership text.

Alton Garrison
Executive Director, Acts 2 Journey Initiative and former Asst. General Superintendent, Assemblies of God USA

Most of us have heard about being in the midst of "the greatest transfer of wealth in history". One article I just read was "Three Ways to Prepare Yourself for the Great Wealth Transfer".

I believe we are also living in the greatest transfer of spiritual and pastoral leadership in the church's history.

It has been reported that one third of all lead pastors are over sixty years of age.

Succession is coming! The question is will we be ready?

Ron's book, *The Transition Leader*, could be the answer. He gives us both principles and examples of church transitions. He shows that if transition is done intentionally, there will be great fruit and the Kingdom of God will advance.

I highly recommend for every church pastor and every church board member to read this book. I will be putting this book in the hands of every North Carolina Assemblies of God pastor.

Transition is coming and I want us all to be ready.

Dr. Rick Ross
North Carolina Assemblies of God Superintendent

Copyright © 2022 by Ron McManus

Published by Dream Releaser Publishing

All rights reserved. No portion of this book may be reproduced, stored in a retrieval system, or transmitted in any form or by any means—electronic, mechanical, photocopy, recording, scanning, or other—except for brief quotations in critical reviews or articles, without prior written permission of the author.

Scripture quotations marked NIV are taken from the Holy Bible, New International Version®, NIV®. Copyright © 1973, 1978, 1984, 2011 by Biblica, Inc.™ Used by permission of Zondervan. All rights reserved worldwide. www.zondervan.com. The "NIV" and "New International Version" are trademarks registered in the United States Patent and Trademark Office by Biblica, Inc.™

For foreign and subsidiary rights, contact the author.

Cover design by: Sara Young

Cover photo by: Andrew van Tilborgh

ISBN: 978-1-959095-30-9   1 2 3 4 5 6 7 8 9 10

Printed in the United States of America

YOUR CHURCH'S KEY TO A
SUCCESSFUL PASTORAL CHANGE

THE
TRANSITION
LEADER

DR. RON McMANUS

This book is dedicated to the memory of my father, Selby F. McManus. Alongside my mom, he faithfully served as a pastor for fifty-five years.

He loved and served the Lord with a humble heart, and he served people faithfully. He refused to let other people determine his value and never allowed anger or resentment to remain in his spirit. He taught me how to love people.

I'm the person I am today because of the investment he made in me. He remains my hero in the faith.

CONTENTS

Foreword xi

   INTRODUCTION *The Inevitable Challenges of Change* 13

PART I. TWO WAYS TO TRANSITION 27

   CHAPTER 1. *"We Need Your Help"* 29

   CHAPTER 2. *Responding to a Sudden Loss* 39

   CHAPTER 3. *Making a Plan* 47

PART II. LEADING THROUGH TRANSITION 51

   CHAPTER 4. *Transition Takes Time and Experience* 53

   CHAPTER 5. *The Transition Leader's Unique Gifting and Calling* 59

   CHAPTER 6. *"The Pause That Refreshes"* 67

   CHAPTER 7. *From "Executive Transition" to "Heart Transplant"* 77

PART III. NAVIGATING THROUGH TRANSITION 89

   CHAPTER 8. *Embarking on the Transition Journey* 91

   CHAPTER 9. *Preaching the Flock Through the Transition* 95

CHAPTER 10. **Leading the Leaders** 105

CHAPTER 11. **Assess to Bless** 119

CHAPTER 12. **The Church Starts Its Search** 129

CHAPTER 13. **The Final Lap** 163

CONCLUSION **Transitioning Through COVID, Post-COVID, and Beyond**....................173

About the Author..179

Foreword

My name is Doug Clay and I have the privilege of serving as General Superintendent of the Assemblies of God, one of the largest Pentecostal denominations in the world. Prior to my current position, I served as treasurer for nine years. Before my time working with the General Council, I was the superintendent of Ohio after pastoring Calvary Assembly of God in Toledo, Ohio.

I have had the opportunity to witness Dr. Ron McManus and his gift of leadership help a multitude of churches with leadership development, consulting, advising, developing processes, walking churches through transitions, and more. Ron has the gift of being able to handle a situation that needs help, carry it through necessary change, and implement healthy wisdom that leaves the church set up to thrive.

Having years of ministry experience and overseeing the denomination I currently serve in, I am passionate about seeing this book reach every pastor, board member, and ministry leader possible.

There is a tsunami that is on its way. It will create church transitions and we will not be ready if we are not careful. Ron has over twenty years of experience in this and is the one who has been the most successful. He shares in this book not only why this will take place but how to handle it when it does.

Many churches are waking up to the reality that their pastor may not be there forever. Fact—every pastor is temporary. Every church will go through a succession or transition... planned or unplanned!

Every year, thousands of churches experience pastoral transition. Church missiologists agree that in the next ten years there will be 480,000 pastoral transitions across America and many of these churches do not have a succession plan. Pastoral transitions are no longer a retirement conversation but a critical readiness conversation.

Ron has written an outstanding book, The Transition Leader. The value of this book is that it is not just written from theory and data but from experience. Ron has led twenty transitions and twelve interim pastorates. His experience and success give him relevancy to this subject like no one else.

INTRODUCTION
The Inevitable Challenges of Change

In June 2022, the pastor of one of America's biggest and most influential churches made an important announcement. Rick Warren, founding pastor and forty-three-year leader of Saddleback Church, was retiring, and the church was transitioning to a new leader.

"We have found God's couple to lead our congregation, and they have agreed to come!" Warren told his flock. The new pastor immediately began attending Saddleback and officially took over as pastor on September 12.

Saddleback's transition process actually began in the summer of 2021 as the sixty-eight-year-old Warren dealt with health problems, including spinal myoclonus, which caused him to experience tremors and blurred vision.

Transitions can be tough, particularly when a pastor has served faithfully for decades, but this high-profile change of leadership at this high-profile church went smoothly because, unlike most churches, Saddleback Church had created a solid transition plan.

Then, suddenly there was a hitch.

OLD ISSUES SURFACE

Before new Saddleback pastor Andy Wood settled into his new pastorate, staff members at his previous church, Echo Church in San Jose, California, aired complaints that Wood had been abusive and created an unhealthy culture in the growing multisite church.

Saddleback went into action, hiring not one but two Christian executive search companies to investigate Wood's tenure at Echo. One company conducted an investigation, the results of which were kept private, and a second company reviewed the first company's work.

As *Christianity Today* reported in July 2022, Saddleback sent an e-mail to twenty thousand congregation members announcing the results of the investigation: "After our work, we concluded there is no systemic or pattern of abuse under Andy's leadership, nor was there an individual that we felt was abused."[1]

A TROUBLED TRANSITION

Saddleback followed a principled, year-long process for its change, and even though the process encountered a few bumps along the way, it was completed successfully. That's a far different scenario than unplanned or sudden transitions, which are frustratingly common.

The scenario was completely different for another big, influential church and its well-known leader. In this case,

---

[1] Bob Smietana, "Search Firm: No Systemic Abuse at Saddleback Successor's Former Church." *Christianity Today*, 14 July 2022, https://www.christianitytoday.com/news/2022/july/saddleback-church-rick-warren-andy-wood-echo-abuse-investig.html.

the forced transition of a beloved founding pastor had led to confusion, the resignation of key leaders, and a significant loss of members.

Bill Hybels founded Willow Creek Community Church, a Chicago, Illinois, megachurch, in the 1970s. By 2017, the "seeker-sensitive" church had twenty-five thousand weekly worshipers and exerted denomination-like influence over thousands of other churches that were part of its Willow Creek Association.

But Hybels was dogged by charges of abuse of power and a series of complaints about misconduct going back twenty years. He denied the allegations, calling them "flat-out lies," but he finally resigned under protest in 2018.[2]

Willow Creek had no transition plan. After Hybels left, new co-pastors were named, but the transition was troubled, and before long, the co-pastors resigned, along with the entire church elder board that had presided over the flawed transition.

In May 2022—one month before Warren announced Saddleback's transition plan—Willow Creek made a more somber announcement. With attendance down 57 percent from 2019, and with giving down, too, Willow Creek announced it would let go of 30 percent of its staff to save $6.5 million in budget expenses. These cuts followed earlier rounds of staff cuts in 2019 and 2020.

---

2 Jerome Socolovky, "Megachurch Pastor Bill Hybels Resigns, Calls Sexual Accusations 'Flat-out Lies'." *Religion News Service*, 14 Apr. 2018, https://religionnews.com/2018/04/11/megachurch-pastor-bill-hybels-resigns-calls-sexual-accusations-flat-out-lies/.

NO PASTORATE LASTS FOREVER

Warren and Hybels both served for decades, but each, in his own way, discovered that nothing—including a pastorate—lasts forever.

Every pastor is temporary.

Every pastor will leave their church, either through a planned succession and transition or through unplanned circumstances or death.

> *Every pastor will leave their church, either through a planned succession and transition or through unplanned circumstances or death.*

In a sense, every pastor is an "interim" pastor.

I've been a successful pastor for decades, so I understand pastors' reluctance to plan for their own replacements. As we will see, there are many reasons that some pastors hang on to leadership for too long, including worries about their personal finances and uncertainty about what they will do next.

When pastors hang on too long, they risk leaving their churches in decline, making it harder for the congregations or the next leaders to turn things around.

It's when pastors leave suddenly—either through illness, sudden death, or moral failure—that many churches realize, too late, that they have no transition plan, so they start this long and challenging process from scratch with little sound guidance.

This book is designed to help you avoid this painful scenario.

PRINCIPLES APPLY TO MINISTRIES TOO

The principles and practices I will be giving you in this book can also be used for transitions in parachurch leadership. As with churches, planned transitions typically work much better than unplanned. One recent transition provides a good example.

On Saturday, September 23, 2022, hundreds of employees, friends, and supporters gathered in Colorado Springs, Colorado, to celebrate a transition that had been in the works for a year but had been discussed for a decade.

Dick Eastman, 78, had been CEO of Every Home for Christ for thirty-four years. According to an article by Steve Rabey, religion correspondent for *The Gazette*, the $60 million ministry works with 12,400 churches in 155 nations and has made gospel presentations in 2.5 billion homes.[3]

Eastman started thinking about the transition a decade earlier but got serious about the change in 2021. That year a plan was approved by EHC's board to replace Eastman with Tanner Peake, who is thirty-eight and has been with the ministry for twelve years. Rabey reports:

---

[3] Steve Rabey, "Every Home for Christ CEO Dick Eastman Passes Leadership Baton after 34 Years," *Colorado Springs Gazette*, 2 Oct. 2022, https://gazette.com/life/every-home-for-christ-ceo-dick-eastman-passes-leadership-baton-after-34-years/article_ad23d6e2-385d-11ed-ab97-0bd826f98642.html.

> *Peake says he plans no major changes but says EHC faces new challenges ... in growing feelings, even among some evangelicals his age, that evangelism is socially divisive or "extreme." Eastman, meanwhile, isn't going anywhere. ... He will stay at EHC as the ministry's chief prayer officer. ... Prayer ... has been central to [Eastman's] work for decades. He launched the Change the World School of Prayer, which has trained more than 2,000,000 Christians in 120 nations in "the power and intimacy of prayer." It is now called the Global Prayer School. His two dozen books on evangelism and intercessory prayer have sold two million copies.*

The transition is a win-win. A new leader can take the ministry into the future while its past leader shores up the prayer support essential to the ministry's success.

TODAY'S TRANSITION TSUNAMI

From the beginning of time, godly leaders have struggled with transitions. In the Old Testament, Moses successfully transferred his leadership to Joshua, under whom Israel experienced prosperity and military victories. But Joshua failed to orchestrate a similar transition, and after his death, Israel slid into immorality and idolatry.

This is a lesson of great urgency for churches facing the challenges of the twenty-first century. A wave of resignations is washing over North American churches. If there were ever a time when churches needed to plan for the future, that time is now.

A March 2022 study from the Barna Group found that 42 percent of pastors were considering resigning.[4] That was up from 29 percent of pastors a year earlier. Barna said the three biggest reasons pastors cited were "immense stress," feelings of isolation and loneliness, and "political division."[5]

Every year, thousands of churches undergo pastoral transitions, and the pace of change is expected to pick up.

During the coming ten years, there are expected to be 480,000 pastoral transitions across America. That represents significant change, but the most worrisome fact is that an astounding 90 percent of these transitions—roughly 430,000—will occur in churches without any succession plan in place.

"There is a tidal wave of Boomer pastors who are about to retire in the next five to 10 years, and there aren't many younger pastors identified to take their place," says Baptist pastor and author Bryant Wright, author of *Succession: Preparing Your Ministry for the Next Leader*. "Most churches don't have a succession plan in place for when the time comes."[6]

As a result of this lack of planning, many of these transitions will go poorly. Many churches will suffer and shrink. Sadly, many believers will grow frustrated and transfer to other churches or, even worse, give up on going to church altogether. Things don't need to happen this way.

---

[4] "Pastors Share Top Reasons They've Considered Quitting Ministry in the Past Year," *Barna Group*, 27 Apr. 2022, https://www.barna.com/research/pastors-quitting-ministry/.
[5] "Pastors Share Top Reasons They've Considered Quitting. . . ."
[6] Bryant Wright, *Succession: Preparing Your Ministry for the Next Leader* (Nashville: B & H Books, 2022).

MY JOURNEY FROM PASTOR TO CHANGE AGENT

I learned all about transitions the hard way after churches started contacting me to help them more than twenty years ago. I had pastored and nurtured Assemblies of God congregations for decades, sticking with my thriving church in Winston-Salem, North Carolina, even as I wrestled with a frightening cancer diagnosis.

It was a joy to receive the loving care of my congregation throughout this challenging time, and I planned to stay at the church as long as I could. But then, a change sought me out.

Pastor and bestselling author John Maxwell called me and asked me to help him start EQUIP, his leadership training company.

Before cancer, I would have turned the offer down and stayed put. But the experience of facing death changes people, and my cancer battle changed my perspective and made me willing to be more of a risk-taker.

As I prayed about Maxwell's offer, and as I read Bob Buford's book *Halftime: Moving from Success to Significance*,[7] I sensed that God was giving me a chance to use my longtime passion for developing Christian leaders. I had long dreamed of helping leaders be better leaders, so I walked away from my church to help other churches.

CRIES FOR HELP CHANGED MY PLANS

As I worked with EQUIP, something strange soon started happening. One church after another contacted me for help

---
[7] Bob Buford, *Half Time: Moving From Success to Significance* (Grand Rapids, MI: Zondervan, 2015).

navigating leadership changes. In one case, I got a call from a worried elder after his megachurch's beloved pastor in his fifties fell over dead one morning at IHOP. In another case, a pastor was gone overnight after revelations of sexual scandal surfaced.

I soon discovered that many churches lacked even a basic plan for transition, which only makes the whole process much more difficult.

In time, I realized what many churches eventually realize. While many search firms offer to help churches find new pastors, there's much more to leadership transition than filling a job vacancy. Without a solid transition plan, these new pastors may face tough sledding.

For the new pastor to succeed, the congregation needs to adjust, heal, and gain a new vision for their future. Church leadership and staff must go through their own processes of adjustment and preparation. A search team needs to be organized and managed.

The more churches I helped, the more I learned about what was needed to make transitions succeed. Before long, it became clear that God had called me to be something I had never known existed years earlier. My calling was to help churches by serving as their Transition Leader.

Now, a dozen churches and a dozen transition processes later, I'm pleased to report that all but one have been successful. These congregations are now healthy and growing, with many surpassing earlier figures for membership, giving, and community impact.

A PLEA TO LEADERS

Even some of the largest churches fail to plan properly for transition. Churches cite many good reasons for their inaction: pressures of the present, poor choices for successors, the inability of current leaders to let go, and other unforeseen challenges.

But Tom Mullins says these excuses aren't good enough, and he challenges leaders to see successful transitions as a final mark of their success as leaders.

"A transition will be one of the greatest tests of your leadership, but it will also serve as one of the greatest rewards and testimonies of your legacy," writes Mullins, author of *Passing the Leadership Baton: A Winning Transition Plan for Your Ministry*.[8] "Successfully handing off the leadership baton to the next leader is essential to give our organization the best opportunity to thrive after our time of service," he writes.[9] And this doesn't happen by accident. A smooth handoff requires forethought, detailed planning, and effective execution.

Some leaders never plan for transitions because they fear the risks that change can bring. But Mullins warns that the risks of *not* planning can be even worse. Mullins focuses on eight action steps, and I will be addressing each one of these in this book:

› Lead through transition.
› Keep the right perspective.

---

[8] Tom Mullins, *Passing the Leadership Baton: A Winning Transition Plan for Your Ministry* (Nashville: Thomas Nelson, 2015).
[9] Mullins, *Passing the Leadership Baton*.

- Prepare for the win.
- Select and prepare your successor.
- Position yourself for success.
- Position others for success.
- Lead through crisis-driven transitions.
- Create a legacy.

Mullins is eloquent in his plea that leaders consider transition as an essential part of their long-term leadership legacy:

Transition really comes down to being an issue of humility and surrender, if you think about it. All the practical things we've discussed in this book have hopefully been helpful to you as you plan with intentionality and troubleshoot inevitable issues along the way to your own transition in leadership.

But the most important thing to consider is the fact God's work is for God's sake—not your own. . . . When that is your realization, it forces you to a place of humility and surrender in the transition process because He alone is the priority, and His plans for His church are what matters above anything else.[10]

The handoff between Tom Mullins and his son Todd is one of the most successful cases of passing the baton in years, and the church continues to grow and be a great model for others to follow.

---

10 Mullins, *Passing the Leadership Baton.*

THE UNIQUE ROLE OF THE TRANSITION LEADER

In studying what makes some changes work while others fail, it didn't take me long to reach a conclusion.

Not only does every church need a *transition plan*, but every church also needs a *Transition Leader* to successfully lead it through the transition process.

In this book, I will guide you, step-by-step, through the whole process, showing how a trained Transition Leader can play a unique role as a buffer between the past and the present. This book is for you if you are:

› A pastor considering your future and the future of your flock.
› The member of a church board that will need to deal with transitions now or in the future.
› Part of the church staff, which is often left in the lurch when changes are made.
› Regional, denominational, or church network leaders responsible for church oversight.

Everything I've written in the pages that follow has been tested and tried multiple times. This book is not theory. It's reality.

> *This book is not theory. It's reality.*

PASSING THE BATON

The apostle Paul wrote about the importance of training and self-discipline in ministry.

Do you not know that in a race all the runners run, but only one gets the prize? Run in such a way as to get the prize. Everyone who competes in the games goes into strict training. They do it to get a crown that will not last, but we do it to get a crown that will last forever."
—1 Corinthians 9:24-25

A crucial part of relay races is the baton pass, when one runner places the baton in the hand of another. Many races are lost when the baton pass is unsuccessful.

No pastorate lasts forever. How will leadership transition happen in your church? Planned and smooth? Or unplanned and unnecessarily harmful?

If you want the process to go smoothly, read on!

PART 1

TWO WAYS TO TRANSITION

CHAPTER 1
"We Need Your Help"

When I see an unfamiliar name and number on my phone, I mentally prepare myself for a heartbreaking conversation.

"Ron, we've had a sudden situation come up with our pastor," an elder or assistant pastor will tell me, "and we need your help."

Over the next few minutes, I find out what has happened and how the church is doing. Next, I ask a crucial question and prepare myself for the predictable answer.

"Well, no, Ron. Our church doesn't really have any kind of transition plan. We're flying blind."

Now I know that the road ahead is going to be more difficult than it needs to be. There are only two ways to transition from one pastor to another:

1) Planned.
2) Unplanned.

Guess which approach most churches take?

IGNORING THE INEVITABLE

People realize that presidents of the United States come and go. Movie stars and musicians face constant competition from younger up-and-coming personalities. A-list athletes age out and retire.

But when it comes to pastors, many of us—including pastors themselves—believe that the status quo will continue, if not forever, at least for a good long while.

We all know better, or at least we should. But in most churches, concerns about what's happening today edge out plans for tomorrow. The inevitable is ignored.

WHY EVERY CHURCH NEEDS A TRANSITION PLAN

The math is indisputable: *100 percent of pastors will stop pastoring at some time.* Whether by choice, circumstance, or death, all pastors will eventually relinquish their position. This is a simple statement of fact, but most pastors and church leaders ignore it, each for their own reasons.

Unfortunately, *90 percent of pastoral transitions occur without any plan.* In life, some things happen by design and some by default. But in the vast majority of churches, leadership change happens by default, meaning there is no plan in place to accommodate succession or transition. In many churches, there are few bylaws that address succession and transition in any meaningful way.

Without a plan, churches are vulnerable. When a pastor announces retirement, suddenly passes away, or experiences a moral failure or catastrophic event, it's up to an unprepared church board to step in, often engaging in a furious process that finds them making things up as they go along.

> *In life, some things happen by design and some by default. But in the vast majority of churches, leadership change happens by default.*

Frequently, people who are forced to confront a sudden pastoral departure feel that they need to act quickly, concluding that the clock is ticking, and the flock is impatient for a new shepherd.

But when time becomes a major factor in recruitment, churches fly through a process that would be better if handled slowly and deliberately. There's more to a successful transition than finding a new pastor. An entire congregation needs to say farewell and possibly heal from the past while preparing to see what God has next for them.

Transitions that happen quickly and focus only on filling the pastoral position don't always work out well. Hasty transitions can leave churches weaker, leading to stagnation, decline, or even death. In my experience, the most successful transitions take between twelve and twenty-four months. Trying to make things happen more quickly can short-circuit the crucial steps needed to ensure the future health of the congregation.

DIFFERENT WAYS TO TRANSITION

There are many ways transitions can happen. Here's an overview that highlights the pros and cons of the various models.

1) Planned Transition

When a pastor and church board are future-oriented, they will establish a plan for the pastor's departure and subsequent successor while he/she is still the lead pastor. Planning ahead allows the pastor and board to create a profile of the ideal candidate and a calendar for leading the congregation through change.

Most pastors who follow this process start planning three to ten years before their projected departure, but they typically don't have a successor in mind.

2) Planned Transition with Transition Leader

Over the last twenty years, I've helped more than a dozen churches navigate pastoral change by serving as their Transition Leader for at least one year. It's a unique calling but a necessary one in many cases. Here's why:
> The Transition Leader can lead the congregation through periods of growth and assessment before initiating the process of finding the new pastor.
> The Transition Leader works with church staff to help them through the process of change.

> The Transition Leader guides church leadership through the process of selecting a new pastor and helps the chosen successor adapt to the new position.

There are risks any time a church faces a leadership transition. The Transition Leader can provide a safe, stable bridge to take a church from the past to the future.

3) Legacy Succession

When a long-term pastor disciples and mentors his own successor, the successor can step into leadership as soon as the pastor steps down or is no longer able to lead, minimizing the congregation's shock and surprise and drastically shortening the transition period. The chosen successor can be the pastor's biological or spiritual son or daughter.

This approach can work well if executed well and given plenty of time. Most legacy transitions involve an outgoing pastor who was a founder of the church or re-founder (someone who took the role of pastor at a time of stagnation or when a church was very small). The new pastor may need time to be established.

But legacy successions can also become messy and easily derailed by family dynamics, conflicts among church leadership, loyalty demands, unrealistic timelines, and members' unmet expectations.

Another challenge: If there are problems or weaknesses in the departing leader's methods or leadership, these problems may be passed on to the next leader rather than being identified and addressed during a normal transition period.

4) Sudden Departures: Unplanned or Catastrophic

Things can happen to our beloved leaders. Sometimes, a pastor ages and loses his edge, necessitating an unplanned change. Other times, a pastor may be felled by physical sickness, mental incapacity, or death. In other cases, a pastor leaves suddenly due to sexual scandal, abuse of power, financial fraud, moral failure, or other illegal activities.

When natural causes force a pastor to leave, congregation members may deal with a range of emotions, including shock, grief, and sorrow. When a pastor falls due to sin or scandal, members may need significant healing and encouragement to overcome their feelings of loss, injustice, anger, and outrage.

5) Transition With Denominational Leader Oversight

In some church denominations and faith traditions, regional or national representatives will help congregations navigate the transition process.

PLANNED TRANSITIONS HAVE BETTER RESULTS THAN UNPLANNED CHANGES

Christian researcher George Barna issued a 2019 report with Brotherhood Mutual called *Leadership Transitions*.[11] Here's what Barna found: "Analysts grouped pastoral successions into three major types based on the circumstances directing the leadership change."

---

[11] "Planned Pastoral Transitions Lead to Better Outcomes," *Barna Group*, 6 Aug. 2019, https://www.barna.com/research/pastoral-transitions/.

1) Planned transitions, planned in advance of the change (17 percent)
2) Pastor-initiated transitions, set into motion by a decision from the outgoing pastor (62 percent)
3) Forced transitions, commenced by unexpected circumstances such as illness, death, or crisis (13 percent).

Barna's team concluded:

When transition is planned in advance, pastoral and leadership staff have time to map out the shift without emotions and lack of time being thrown into the equation. This approach is more likely to lead to positive outcomes once all is said and done. In general, churches where the pastor departs entirely—most common in unplanned transitions—have more tumultuous outcomes. As you might expect, pastors who depart entirely are most likely to move on to pastor another church (34 percent).

Half of incoming pastors say there was no plan before the previous pastor began to transition out (51 percent). In addition, one-third of incoming pastors reports that a lack of planning created extreme difficulty (12 percent) or major obstacles (21 percent) to achieving a smooth and successful transition. Taken together, these data drive home one of the big takeaways from this research: If you can, plan. Planning ahead can smooth the leadership shift and produce more positive outcomes for everyone involved. As emotions often run hot during a season of change, the more decisions made beforehand or outside the heat of the moment, the better.

THE POWER OF A PLAN

Change happens. No leader lasts forever. The best way to prepare is to have a plan.

> *The best way to prepare is to have a plan.*

Let's look at two cases—one planned and one not—in the next two chapters.

> **Transition: By Design or by Default?**
>
> Leadership consultant Sam Chand has helped many churches and organizations improve their leaders' effectiveness and plan for leadership transitions. He has helped lead transitions that have gone well, and he has been called to help out when they go poorly. Chand sees planning and preparation as the key factor determining success or failure.
>
> Chand explains the importance of planning in his book Tsunami:
>
> > *Life happens. Death happens. Unfortunate circumstances incapacitate leaders. We've all heard of sudden death, long-term debilitating illness, moral failure, deviance from doctrine and mission, and unforeseen resignations. Most organizations do not have a plan or a process to deal with*

> such catastrophes. In these situations, intervention is necessary to provide for a transitional Pastor or replacement candidate. This is especially critical when there is no succession plan in place.

As a church leader, can you think of a church pastoral succession or transition that went badly? Knowing what you know, what could have averted that? How long did the fallout continue? How many people left the church and never went back?

> **Can you think of a church pastoral succession or transition that went well? We would suggest that the primary difference between the two is that the one that went badly was done by default, and the one that went well was done by design.**

Now let's look at the other side of the spectrum. Can you think of a church pastoral succession or transition that went well? I would suggest that the primary difference between the two is that the one that went badly was done by *default*, and the one that went well was done by *design*. Statistics point to the inevitable transition I mentioned in the introduction—nearly half a million experienced pastors retiring from their pulpits over the next ten years. Considering that the vast majority have no succession plan in place, we very well could be looking at a problem of staggering proportions.

CHAPTER 2
Responding to a Sudden Loss

Bob Schmidgall was just out of Bible college when he founded Calvary Temple in Naperville, Illinois, in 1967. Under his leadership, the church grew, rapidly outgrowing three locations, adding a school and children's center, and giving significant funds for church mission programs.

Thirty-one years later, Bob was still leading Calvary (now known as Calvary Church of Naperville). But suddenly, on January 6, 1998, everything changed.

Pastor Bob was meeting staff for breakfast at an IHOP restaurant when he fell over at his table and died instantly of heart failure. He was fifty-five and in good health.

Bob was a great leader and shepherd of his flock. He had grown this church from eight families to two thousand members. His congregation loved him. His sudden loss was a major blow.

"What's Calvary without Bob?" some asked.

Church leadership felt the same way. Elders had no idea how to proceed.

"We really need your help, Ron," the head of the church board told me.

When I asked the board member if the church had a transition plan, he hemmed and hawed before admitting the sad truth.

"We didn't think we would need any plan," he told me. "Bob was still so young. It seemed he would be here forever."

Pastoral Transition 101

I got the desperate call from Calvary after I had started working with John Maxwell at EQUIP. Although I had been a pastor for decades, I didn't know much about the process of transitioning a church from one leader to the next. I wasn't alone.

I've heard many pastors talk about "ending well," but few give as much time or attention to planning how they will "pass the baton" to the next generation of leaders.

Pastors think about transition, but the subject makes many uncomfortable, and few discuss it with church leadership.

It's equally rare for church boards to bring it up unless they see obvious signs of decline.

Now I was about to see what a sudden and unplanned transition process looked like from the inside.

My experience would open my eyes to a vast, unaddressed challenge going on in churches across the country that was eating away at the health of Christ's body. My experience would also reveal my new calling: leading congregations through the challenges of change.

FREQUENT FLYER

I heard about Bob's death from my friend Dick Foth, who knows many leaders through his work with The Fellowship in Washington, DC. Dick was close to the people at Calvary and asked me to consider lending a hand.

"Is there any way you can help them out?" he asked me.

When the church officially called me and asked me to fly to Naperville, so I could be in the church's pulpit the next Sunday morning, I was ready to say yes.

That's how it all began. I agreed to preach at Naperville the next Sunday. And the next Sunday. And the next Sunday. I would be flying from Atlanta to Naperville every weekend for the next two years.

A godly preacher tries to feel what a congregation is feeling. That first Sunday, I encountered a deep well of grief and sorrow, and in my sermon, I tried to bring the healing and hope that can be found in Christ.

BECOMING A "TRANSITION LEADER"

I soon saw that my role at Naperville would involve much more than ministering to the grieving congregation. Before I knew it, I was becoming a Transition Leader even though, at the time, I didn't know there was such a thing.

Serving Church Leaders

Bob's death was hard on church members, but church leaders seemed to suffer even more. On top of their grief was their shock at suddenly being forced to make major decisions they were not prepared to tackle. These leaders needed healing for their hurts. At the same time, they had to be resilient in the face of this tragedy because their brothers and sisters in Christ needed them to be strong and decisive.

Thankfully, Calvary had a great executive pastor and a wonderful chief financial officer who helped stabilize the team. Soon, I was adding half a day to my weekly commute, so I could meet with these and other Calvary leaders in Naperville.

Helping Church Staff

Bob's death was hard on church leaders and church staff too. They felt sorrow, sadness, insecurity about the future, and pressure to measure up.

In some churches, the sudden disappearance of a pastor leads to chaos and anxiety. Sometimes it seems like everyone is in charge, and other times, it seems like no one is in charge. Some staff worry about losing their jobs under a new administration.

Fortunately, Calvary had a great Executive Pastor, Keith Boucher, and CFO, Mark Bergan, that provided solid leadership throughout the transition.

The Search

The church faced an obvious need. Who would be the new leader? They asked me if I would like to succeed Bob, but I already had a good job and didn't want to return to being a full-time pastor. However, I knew I could help the church board find a new pastor.

I didn't want to rush that process, though. Pastor Bob had founded this church and led it for three decades. This church needed more than a new pastor. It needed a new vision for its future.

Within a few months, this is what my weekly calendar looked like:

› Arrive Saturday for Sunday morning church services.
› Lead Sunday evening board meetings.
› Lead Monday morning meetings with the executive team and fly home

Step by step, I was learning what Calvary needed and figuring out how I could help them successfully navigate the process. Somewhere along the way, I discovered a new calling and, with it, a new job title: Transition Leader.

The Transition Leader walks alongside a church in transition, helping people grieve, heal, figure out their calling, articulate their vision for the future, and find the pastor who can help them make it all happen.

> **The Transition Leader walks alongside a church in transition, helping people grieve, heal, figure out their calling, articulate their vision for the future, and find the pastor who can help them make it all happen.**

DEFINING SUCCESS

At first, I had no idea I would commute to Naperville for two years, but once I began walking alongside this grieving congregation, I could see what they needed at each step along the way.

When I started helping them, I didn't really have a good definition of success. Now I do, and it's found on Calvary's website:

> After a two-year search, the church elected Pastor Randal Ross in 2000. Under Pastor Ross' passionate, spirit-led leadership, Calvary's attendance grew in size and diversity.[12]

And because of Pastor Randall's vision to reach the community, the church added new campuses, including an Indian ministry (now a church), and Spanish-speaking Calvary en Español.

With the benefit of hindsight, I would call that a successful transition.

NO TRANSITION IS 100 PERCENT SUCCESSFUL

Even the most successful transitions can be stressful for all involved. Steve Rabey of *The Gazette*, writes:

> Pastors come and pastors go, and even when handled well, such transitions can cause disorientation, anxiety, grief, and even trauma for church members, says Bob Kaylor, a Monument [Colorado] pastor who helps churches undergo leadership changes.

---
12 "Our Story," *Calvary Church of Naperville - Our Story*, https://calvarynaperville.org/history.

"Pastoral transitions are times of acute vulnerability for congregations," says Kaylor, author of *Your Best Move: Effective Leadership Transition for the Local Church.*[13]

"And the stakes are higher the bigger the church."

When handled well, pastoral transitions can energize a church, says Kaylor, the lead pastor of Tri-Lakes United Methodist Church in Monument.

But it's not unusual for attendance and giving to decline by 15 percent. And when the process is handled poorly, or when a pastor has left due to moral failure or a church schism, the transition can be jarring and destructive.

Few church leaders receive specialized training in leadership transitions. That's why Kaylor leads workshops on the subject. He wrote his book to guide elder boards and transition teams through the process.[14]

FROM ONE SUCCESS TO ANOTHER

My experience at Naperville changed my understanding of what transitions could be and how they could succeed. Soon enough, I would be using everything I learned in Illinois to help a transition in California.

---

13 Robert Kaylor, *Your Best Move: Effective Leadership Transition for the Local Church* (Wilmore, KY: Seedbed Publishing, 2013).
14 Steve Rabey, "Pastors on the Move: Getting through a Time of Change at Colorado Springs-Area Churches," *Colorado Springs Gazette*, 24 Nov. 2013, https://gazette.com/life/pastors-on-the-move-getting-through-a-time-of-change-at-colorado-springs-area-churches/article_b16afa95-40b2-5775-97c6-a109f6a0f142.html.

CHAPTER 3
Making a Plan

After two years of commuting to Calvary, I was ready to spend time anywhere—except airports. But after a brief two-week hiatus, an unknown name and number showed up on my phone.

"Ron, I need your help."

It was a megachurch pastor I had known for years.

"I've got a birthday coming up in six months," he told me. "I want you to help me pass leadership on to our next leader."

I was relieved this transition wouldn't be a sudden, unplanned one like Naperville. But there was one complicating twist.

"Ron, over the years I've promised just about all of my assistants that they would be my chosen successor, and probably a dozen or more of these folks may be upset if they aren't chosen."

Thus began my weekly commutes to Fresno, California.

A WAR OVER SUCCESSION

By the time he retired from the church after forty-five years as pastor, G. L. Johnson had built the small congregation into a four thousand-member megachurch with a K-12 Christian school.

Now nearing eighty and looking forward to retirement, he told me that his looming resignation was also a source of anxiety. As he explained to me, he had been a loving mentor who had guided the growth of many church leaders. Along the way, he had led many of these devoted servants to believe that they would be named the new church leader if he ever left. Many of these supposed heirs to the pulpit were on the church staff, which created challenges at first.

We decided that the only way to treat everyone fairly was to mandate that anyone who wanted to be considered for the senior pastor position should let the search committee know. We also made it clear that any internal candidates who were not selected would need to leave the church after the decision was made, so they wouldn't sow division or fight the transition.

STAYING TOO LONG

G. L. was still plenty sharp at 79.5 years old, but as he acknowledged to me many times, he should have started planning for his successor a quarter century earlier.

He's far from alone. Many pastors stay too long. Why do they do it?

- For some, the concern is financial: "How will I earn my living now?"
- For others, it's more emotional: "How can the church I birthed and nurtured for decades survive without me?"
- For others, transition raises deeper anxieties about meaning and purpose. Many wonder: What's my next calling? What's my purpose in life now?
- For others, it's a simple issue of waiting for a perfect time that never comes: "I don't want to give them any ideas about me leaving until I'm ready to leave."

PLANNING MAKES ALL THE DIFFERENCE

Even with its unusual plot twists, the transition at the church went well, thanks in part to the two-year transition process we put in place that would honor and celebrate Pastor Johnson's lengthy service while welcoming a new shepherd of the flock. You need to let go before you can move on.

As you might imagine, the grieving process was long and deep for some members as they bade farewell to their spiritual father. But their wise choice of his successor allayed any remaining fears.

As *The Fresno Bee* reported at the time:

The congregation of Peoples Church in northeast Fresno is feeling a sense of excitement.

March 14 is the Rev. Dale Oquist's first Sunday as senior pastor of the church, one of the central San Joaquin Valley's largest congregations.

> Oquist, senior pastor of Evergreen Christian Community in Olympia, Wash., for the past 10 years, replaces the Rev. G.L. Johnson, who retired in February 2008 after nearly 45 years as the church's pastor.[15]

Thirteen years later, the church is still thriving, and Dale is still pastor.

---

[15] Ron Orozco, "New Pastor Begins at Peoples Church," *The Fresno Bee*, 12 Mar. 2010, https://www.fresnobee.com/article19503927.html.

PART 2
LEADING THROUGH TRANSITION

CHAPTER 4

Transition Takes Time and Experience

The emergency call came in to flight controllers on Tuesday, May 10, 2022.

"I've got a serious situation here," said the man, who was a passenger on a flight from the Bahamas to Florida. "My pilot has gone incoherent. He is out."

As the flight controllers coached the man on how to steady the plane and prepare for a landing, he confessed his ignorance. "I have no idea how to stop the airplane," he said. "I don't know how to do anything."

But the flight controllers remained calm, providing the man with the guidance he needed to land the plane.

This was a successful and sudden transition from experienced pilot to inexperienced passenger. With help, the man was able to avoid catastrophe. Not all transitions happen so rapidly or smoothly, as leaders of one Tennessee church realized.

TWO STRIKES

When the senior pastor of a two thousand-member church left to pastor another church, leaders were confident they could quickly handle the transition to the next pastor.

"We can just put our top associate pastor in the pulpit the next Sunday and avoid all the hassle and expense of a long search," said one of the church elders to agreement from the other leaders.

The associate pastor had been at the church for many years and had developed a loyal following, but he was never as popular as the senior pastor he was replacing, as the church learned one fateful Sunday a few months later.

On the Sunday when the church held a special meeting for members to vote on naming the associate as the new senior pastor, he failed to secure the nomination by four votes, leading to chaos in the church and the eventual departure of the associate pastor. He founded a new church down the road, which soon attracted five hundred members of his previous church.

Even though the two top pastors had left in the span of a few months, church leaders were undaunted and quickly came up with a plan.

"We can get a pastor through pulpit supply and get him in the pulpit right away," one elder suggested. The others agreed, and within two weeks, the new plan was in place.

Four months later, leaders felt certain their new interim pastor had done well enough and endeared himself to the members that they decided they were ready to hold another vote on whether to make him their new senior pastor. The appointed Sunday came. Another vote was taken. And once again, the church was in chaos. The interim pastor lost the election by one vote. Additional tensions ensued, and before long, another five hundred loyal members had grown frustrated and gradually wandered off to other churches—or to no church.

MEET THE TRANSITION LEADER

The troubles at this church in Tennessee show how complicated transitions can be and how destructive they can be when they go wrong.

After seeing too many scenarios like this one, I've become even more convinced that the best way for a church to transition is with the help of a trained and experienced Transition Leader who has already learned these important lessons:

> - Transitions take time, usually from twelve to twenty-four months.
> - Transitions involve much more than simply hiring a new pastor. Changes in pastoral leadership impact virtually every other aspect of a congregation.
> - The Transition Leader serves as a transitional or interim pastor until the permanent pastor is in place, preventing mistakes like those made in Tennessee.
> - The Transition Leader also helps church staff, leaders, and members adjust, recover from the departure of their former pastor, and prepare to welcome their next pastor as he leads the church into the future.

PAYING HONOR AND RESPECT

The guiding passion for the Transition Leader can be summed up in one word: honor. Transitions succeed when we honor all parties involved, no matter where they are on the organizational chart.

> *The guiding passion for the Transition Leader can be summed up in one word: honor.*

Honor up. We respect both the historical legacy of the departing pastor and the calling of the incoming pastor.

Honor down. We show respect for every single member of the congregation, regardless of whether they are leaders or large givers.

Honor all around. We reach out to and include all stakeholders, whether they are members, elders, staff members, volunteer Sunday school teachers, musicians, or greeters.

Through it all, we remind people that transitions are much more than a tale of two pastors—one leaving and one coming on board. Transitions are about being good stewards of the body of Christ. Our goal is a healthy, vibrant, thriving church.

If we simply install an available candidate without establishing healthy systems for the congregation's future, we're being poor stewards of all Christ has done.

THE TRANSITION LEADER'S UNIQUE SKILLS AND EXPERIENCE

What kind of person makes a good Transition Leader? It's a complicated skill set that can be boiled down to a few specific professional qualifications and a handful of essential skills. I know because I work with a number of these peculiar people!

Proven Track Record

First and foremost, we look for someone who has successfully served as a pastor of one or more churches. That's the baseline. The apostle Paul told Timothy, "Don't let anyone look down on you because you are young" (1 Timothy 4:12). But the successful Transition Leader has the wisdom that comes with experience.

Been There, Done That

Second, we want someone who has successfully overseen a transition in pastoral leadership—either at his or her own church or somewhere else.

Only One Agenda

The fact that the Transition Leader doesn't want to be (and is actually prevented from being) the church's next leader is a valuable asset. This makes things simpler. The only goal is successfully leading the church through the transition—not landing a job.

Like I tell people early on, "Look, I'm here for you and for Christ. I don't really have a dog in this fight. I have no agenda other than helping you prepare for your next leader."

Down but Not Out

Finally, the job favors someone who has already previously "hit the wall" and bounced back. The ideal candidate is someone who has already successfully dealt with the many stresses and strains that threaten the stability of many pastors but has not been crippled or burned out by these experiences. We need someone who has not only been tried and tested but has also been transformed by the power of the Holy Spirit.

> We need Transition Pastors who have not only been tried and tested but have also been transformed by the power of the Holy Spirit.

HELP WANTED

Does my brief portrayal of the Transition Leader sound like something you could see yourself doing? If so, you may be fortunate due to those hundreds of thousands of churches that will go through leadership transitions in the coming years. As we have seen, few of them are as prepared as they should be for the challenges to come.

In the next chapter, we'll explore those challenges and show how the Transition Leader navigates them one by one.

CHAPTER 5

The Transition Leader's Unique Gifting and Calling

The apostle Paul gave the young leader Timothy a mini-lesson about the characteristics he should embody as a pastor:

Set an example for the believers in speech, in conduct, in love, in faith and in purity. Until I come, devote yourself to the public reading of Scripture, to preaching and to teaching. Do not neglect your gift, which was given you through prophecy when the body of elders laid their hands on you. —1 Timothy 4:12-14

If I were writing a mini-lesson about the characteristics of the Transition Leader, it might go something like this:

Churches in transition need someone who can "feel the pain" of losing their trusted shepherd. You may be a brilliant theologian and a gifted communicator, but if you lack love and a bit of emotional intelligence, you may wind up hurting instead of healing. The Transition Leader knows a church is more than an "institution" undergoing change. Christ's church is a living spiritual body we must nurture and strengthen.

Churches undergoing transition face instability and challenges that can hurt the flock. They need firm but gentle pastoral leadership as they navigate their way from yesterday to tomorrow. Here's a complete list of the characteristics needed for this most unusual and important assignment.

> **Churches undergoing transition face instability and challenges that can hurt the flock. They need firm but gentle pastoral leadership as they navigate their way from yesterday to tomorrow.**

Confidentiality

Many uncomfortable and sensitive issues arise in the process of developing a succession plan. Trust is essential, and trust comes when people know their secrets are safe with you. All information, discussions, and plans will remain confidential and won't be discussed with people who aren't involved without explicit permission. A Transition Leader is someone who has learned to control the tongue and can share that gift with others.

Deep Listening

The Transition Leader does more than "hear what you say" and actually "understands what you mean." We listen to the unspoken language of the heart to discern people's pain and fear and intuitively navigate through tough conversations and challenging situations. The only school that teaches this gift is experience, including years spent guiding difficult conversations appropriately.

Cultural Sensitivity

Every church has its own DNA, history, and organizational culture. The Transition Leader respectfully operates within that context, paying due respect for the many milestones passed while also preparing for challenges yet to come. I continually ask, *Lord, what have You called this congregation to do? And who have You called to lead them?*

Customized Process

No two transitions are the same. That's why the process that worked in Church A may fail at Church B. A successful leadership transition requires a fully customized plan and process for each church.

Seeking Out Sensitive Conversations

In many churches, unsettled or difficult issues can be easily overlooked and left to develop into full-blown problems. Periods of transition are good times to tackle these difficult discussions up front and help settle contentious issues that threaten the success of the next leader. It is better to have these difficult conversations at the very beginning of the process than to avoid them and have larger issues to deal with later that affect the process or organization.

Implementing Transition Processes

I work overtime to engage with the lead pastor, board, staff, and eventually the search committee to develop, promote, and implement the transition plan.

Financially Blessing the Departing Pastor

Some pastors hang on too long simply because they need the income. If a church can provide finances that help an outgoing pastor transition to their next ministry challenge, the departure will likely be sweeter.

Ongoing Guidance

I don't suddenly disappear once the new leader is brought on board and preaches his/her first Sunday sermon. The Transition Leader's assignment continues for the next and final six months of the transition process. This six-month period is the time to make sure that the succeeding pastor is actually succeeding, that the church's many stakeholders are positively engaged, and that the church is growing into its next chapter.

Continuous engagement and presence allow the transition to continue as the new pastor and his flock get to know each other better and, together, address the many challenges that will inevitably come their way.

IS A TRANSITION LEADER THE SAME THING AS AN INTERIM PASTOR?

Different Christian denominations and faith traditions use a variety of practices and language to describe their transition processes.

In some cases, churches bring in denomination-approved interims who handle the preaching and pastoral leadership duties until new pastors are found. In most cases, denominations prohibit these interim pastors from becoming the new leaders—an approach that helps keep things orderly.

Interims typically serve one to two years. In his article, "Pastors on the move: Getting through a time of change at Colorado Springs-area churches," Steve Rabey describes the view of Rick Foster, who has served as an interim for Baptist congregations:

> Foster... compares the interim pastor's role to that of the trail boss on a wagon train. "You look out ahead, you know where you're going, you use the whip on the oxen, and if necessary, the people, and you take a few arrows in the process."[16]

In one case, Foster served a historic church "which had nearly 700 members during its heyday in the 1970s but now serves about 60 members." Eventually, the church decided to deed its large building to a new, growing church that had no permanent facility. The new church has continued to grow, offering programs for people who struggle with addictions and other problems.

---

[16] Steve Rabey, "Pastors on the Move: Getting through a Time of Change."

Rabey finishes his article by quoting Foster:
I am absolutely convinced that the only hope for the world and for people's lives is what the church has to offer, which is the good news of Jesus Christ.... My passion and vision is to be a catalyst for churches in transition to experience a new level of spiritual health.

LEADING FOR JUST A SEASON

Most leaders seek out positions of power that will last for many years, but the fact remains that every pastor is an interim pastor, as Bryant Wright explains to Lifeway Research:

If any church is going to last (and you sure hope it is), you realize that church is going to be around a whole lot longer than the tenure of any pastor. Pastors are given a stewardship where God entrusts the leadership of a church and a congregation to us. It's for a period of time. It's healthier to see ourselves as interim pastors wanting to make the most of that role and lead faithfully in God's will in that interim as long as He allows.[17]

> **The Transition Leader seeks a position of service that lasts only for a very special time in the life of one church body.**

---

[17] Carol Pipes, "How to Pass the Baton to the next Pastor: A Q&A with Bryant Wright," *Lifeway Research*, 5 July 2022, https://research.lifeway.com/2022/07/05/how-to-pass-the-baton-to-the-next-pastor/.

The Transition Leader seeks a position of service that lasts only for a very special time in the life of one church body. The characteristics described here help make transitions successful.

CHAPTER 6
"The Pause That Refreshes"

It doesn't happen very often, but when it does, it's a beautiful thing to see. I'm referring to that occasion when a departing leader personally appoints his successor, and everything works out smoothly.

The Bible paints a picture of such a transition:

*Moses said to the L*ORD*, "May the L*ORD*, the God who gives breath to all living things, appoint someone over this community to go out and come in before them, one who will lead them out and bring them in, so the L*ORD*'s people will not be like sheep without a shepherd."*

*So the L*ORD *said to Moses, "Take Joshua son of Nun, a man in whom is the spirit of leadership, and lay your hand on him. Have him stand before Eleazar the priest and the entire assembly and commission him in their presence. Give him some of your authority so the whole Israelite community will obey him. He is to stand before Eleazar the priest, who will obtain decisions for him by inquiring of the Urim before the L*ORD*. At his command he and the entire community of the Israelites will go out, and at his command they will come in."*

> Moses did as the LORD commanded him. He took Joshua and had him stand before Eleazar the priest and the whole assembly. Then he laid his hands on him and commissioned him, as the LORD instructed through Moses. —Numbers 27:15-23

This commissioning ceremony beautifully symbolized the direct transition from one godly leader to another. Such one-to-one transitions are extremely rare in churches today, and many denominations forbid them. As a result, most congregations will go through a complex process that will wind up lasting between one and two years.

Experience has taught me that a trained Transition Leader can help shaken sheep along the pathway as they find their next shepherd.

A NECESSARY BUFFER BETWEEN PAST AND FUTURE

As America recovered from the economic depression of 1929, Coca-Cola was marketed with this slogan: "The Pause That Refreshes."

You can use that same slogan to describe the role of the Transition Leader. He or she serves as a necessary buffer between the leadership of the past and the leadership of the future.

Many church folk seem to believe that when it comes to transitions, quicker is better. I can understand why they feel that way. When the shepherd is gone, the sheep can feel confused and unsteady. They want to move on as soon as possible, viewing any intermission between past and present as an uncomfortable halt in the process.

But as we've seen, leadership transitions mean much more than simply replacing Pastor A with Pastor B. Leaders are not easily replaced components that can be switched in and out in an instant. Each one is unique.

When you don't have a Moses-to-Joshua handoff, a buffer is better.

RUSHING THE HANDOFF

The thing that makes the 4x100-meter relay so difficult is the handoff. There are four sprinters but only one baton, and it must be passed from runner to runner quickly and in accordance with the rules as runners are racing around the track as fast as humanly possible.

One challenge is that the runner passing the baton does so "blind," meaning it's up to the runner who will receive the baton to grab it.

Another challenge is the passing zone, the thirty-meter-long area on the track where one sprinter passes the baton to the sprinter coming up from behind. The sprinter who carries the baton cannot touch it once he or she leaves the passing zone. The sprinter who is to receive the baton cannot touch it before entering the zone.

When the baton is passed smoothly, the 4x100 race is a thing of beauty, with the four runners pooling their talents to run at a faster clip than they do on their own. But when the handoff is bungled, the runners see their chances for victory slipping away.

Disqualifications are surprisingly common in relay races. Some runners drop batons during the handoff, making it impossible to win the race. Others fail to carry out the switch-off in the passing zone and suffer a penalty.

I've seen too many churches try to rush the handoff from one leader to the next. When this happens, there's more to be lost than a race. Failed leadership handoffs can weaken or even destroy decades-old churches.

PROBLEMS IN PASSING THE BATON

Bryant Wright was the long-term pastor of Johnson Ferry Baptist Church in Marietta, Georgia. Wright's book *Succession*, traces the handoff in his church, beginning with his first mention of his succession plan to the congregation and continuing through the final sermon he preached.

An interviewer asked Wright what kept some churches from successfully passing the leadership baton.

> *Number one, the senior pastor, the long-tenured pastor doesn't have a clear ending date and has a hard time letting go. That's usually a major reason why it doesn't go well.*
>
> *Second, the retiring senior pastor isn't supportive of the pastor who's following him. Thirdly, the wife of the retiring senior pastor has a hard time letting go. Fourth, the successor doesn't show proper respect and honor to the long-tenured pastor they're following.*[18]

---

18 Carol Pipes, "How to Pass the Baton to the next Pastor: A Q&A with Bryant Wright."

WHEN THE PREVIOUS PASTOR HOLDS ON TO THE BATON

Some pastors want to pass most of the baton while holding on to a bit of it for themselves. This typically doesn't work out very well.

Researcher George Barna says most pastors transition entirely out of their congregation. Barna researchers looked at three *directions* of pastoral transition:

First, there are pastors who step back from the senior pastor role and move into a co-pastor or associate pastor role (15 percent).

Second, there are pastors who withdraw from the senior pastor role into lay leadership, such as eldership or teaching, or regular membership in the congregation (a majority of the time, the impetus for moving in this direction is a pastor's retirement) (20 percent).

Thirdly, there are pastors who depart the congregation entirely (56 percent).

As Barna concludes:

Across the board, departing entirely is the most common transitional direction, but it's more common when the transition is unplanned. When a transition is planned in advance, more than half of outgoing pastors stick around, whether they step back to continue on staff or withdraw to a lay role.[19]

---

[19] "Planned Pastoral Transitions Lead to Better Outcomes," *Barna Group*, 6 Aug. 2019, https://www.barna.com/research/pastoral-transitions/.

FINDING OUT TOO LATE

Transitions can go sideways when a church has no built-in buffer between past and future leaders.

After serving at a church in Grand Rapids, Michigan, for twenty-five years, the lead pastor of this thriving megachurch realized it was time for him to move on. He resigned, and church leaders began searching for an immediate replacement.

They quickly found a highly regarded candidate from the West Coast and hired him ASAP. It didn't take long for the congregation to realize that their new leader was a major contrast to their past leader. Some of the changes were cultural. The departing pastor followed a traditional program-driven ministry model tailored to meet the conservative expectations of Grand Rapids's Dutch Reformed community.

More importantly, the departing pastor had spent twenty-five years in this one church while the new pastor was a church planter who was more accustomed to starting a new church and then moving on a few years later after the congregation was established. Both men were pastors, but their callings and experiences were very different.

Many church planters are entrepreneurial. Some are accustomed to starting fresh with new churches rather than dealing with some of the problems that can accumulate in older churches. In many ways, long-term pastors and church planters have different callings and different missions.

The church thought it could do a rapid transition between two different kinds of leaders, but the congregation was caught unaware by the difference between the departing pastor's philosophy of ministry and the new leader's very different philosophy of ministry and congregational experience.

As often happens during a transition, some members leave, taking their donations with them. When this happened in Grand Rapids, some leaders grew concerned about these negative trends in giving.

In his defense, the new pastor accomplished much good. He helped change the church's paradigm, preparing the congregation for its future ministry. But after three years, the new pastor was gone, and the church was back where it started—looking for a pastor—but it now had fewer members and resources to offer.

I was called to step in as the Transition Leader and served this church for the next ten months. We were able to stabilize the congregation, which elected Sam Rijfkogel as their new pastor. He continues to serve today, more than a decade later.

SAYING FAREWELL BEFORE YOU SAY HELLO

Faithward, a reform group affiliated with the Reformed Church in America, published a "Pastoral Transition Survival Guide" which includes a crucial step that many churches skip.

"Take time to process your pastor's departure and say goodbye," says Grace Ruiter.[20] This is an important step

---

[20] Grace Ruiter, "Pastoral Transition Survival Guide: How to Navigate a Pastoral Search and Transition," *Faithward.org*, 18 May 2021, https://www.faithward.org/pastoral-transition-survival-guide-how-to-navigate-a-pastoral-search-and-transition/.

that addresses some of the underlying emotions believers experience when undergoing a transition. Ruiter, guided by the *Reformed Church in America Pastoral Search Handbook*[21] further explains:

> Church members will need to process their feelings about the departing pastor. Dealing with grief is often overlooked, yet it is essential if a church is to move into the search process with a healthy mindset.
>
> Many individuals will express their feelings to the pastor on their own. But you'll want to find appropriate ways to say farewell to your church's departing pastor as a congregation as well. Consider holding a reception or dinner for your church to express thanks and say goodbye to the pastor.

NO BUFFER, CHURCHES SUFFER

I could recite many similar scenarios from other rushed transitions that forced believers to quickly switch not only to different leaders but also to differing ministry styles. Each situation was different, but the outcome was the same, leading me to develop this simple motto: When there's no buffer, churches suffer.

> ### When there's no buffer, churches suffer.

---

21 *Reformed Church in America*, 2020, http://images.rca.org/docs/leadership/PastoralSearchHandbookUpdate.pdf.

I said above that the Transition Leader provides a pause that refreshes, but that really understates the case. There's more at stake here than a soft drink or the momentary relief of thirst.

Transitions are challenging, and even when well-planned and orchestrated, challenges can arise.

An experienced Transition Leader can help churches avoid bungled baton transitions that can turn victory into defeat. With God's blessings and the prayers of the people, a Transition Leader can be an important buffer that prepares church members for potential changes in personal style, ministry philosophy, and church mission.

CHAPTER 7

From "Executive Transition" to "Heart Transplant"

It was the biggest CEO transition in corporate America in years. In 2021, Jeff Bezos named a new CEO to replace him at Amazon, the online book company he founded in 1994 and which now sells everything.

Bezos named Andy Jassy, who led Amazon Web Services, as the new CEO of Amazon, which had revenue of $116 billion in the first quarter of 2022.[22] Now Bezos can focus on his many other priorities, including *The Washington Post* and the space exploration company Blue Origin.

I often hear church board members wishing they could handle pastoral transitions with businesslike efficiency, just like big corporations handle CEO transitions.

But churches aren't corporations. They're living parts of Christ's body. And pastors aren't corporate CEOs. They're

---

[22] "Amazon.com Announces First Quarter Results," *Amazon.com, Inc.*, 28 Apr. 2022, https://ir.aboutamazon.com/news-release/news-release-details/2022/Amazon.com-Announces-First-Quarter-Results-f0188db95/default.aspx#:~:text=Common%20shares%20outstanding%20plus%20shares,billion%20in%20first%20quarter%202021.

devoted shepherds of Christ's flock with unique personalities and ministry approaches.

Even when churches follow the step-by-step approach I lay out in the next part of this book, pastoral transitions aren't always businesslike or efficient. Nor should they be.

When a church changes pastors, there's more going on than a simple executive transition. It's more like a heart transplant. When the pastor, the heart of the local congregation, leaves, it takes time and healing for the body to recover and return to health.

The Transition Leader can play an essential role, giving churches the time they need to transition from past to future, and with God's help, bringing the healing many congregations need before they can move forward.

This healing process is the vital medication that churches need for a successful transplant.

The Transition Leader does more than oversee the replacement of one leader with another. Perhaps most importantly, the Transition Leader guides all the various sheep in the flock through powerful emotions—grief, anxiety, or worse—that accompany even the most successful transition.

The rockier the transition, the more time and healing are needed.

> *The rockier the transition, the more time and healing are needed.*

THE LONG AND SHORT OF TRANSITION

Some pastors stay in the pulpit too long and then make matters worse by digging in their heels and slowing down the transition process once it finally starts. As we've seen, pastors have many motives for moving slowly, including financial anxieties, a need for public gratification, or the absence of any other passion, interest, or calling in life.

Christ's sheep can suffer when His shepherds stay on too long for all the wrong reasons. I see the harm most clearly in the loss of vision for the future. Good leaders always look forward, developing a vision for how the church can thrive.

People can tell when a leader is hanging on rather than moving on: Sometimes. a leader's memories are bigger than their dreams. Other times, a leader is looking longingly in the rear-view mirror instead of keeping an eye on tomorrow. The only time I've ever seen the transition process get sped up was when one church's younger members (meaning those under forty-five!) started referring to their leader as Grandpa, not Pastor.

No amount of external pressure could budge this stubborn old preacher, but when he realized in his heart of hearts that he was no longer effective at reaching and teaching the next generation of believers, he filed away his old sermon notes and started the search for his successor.

On the other extreme, some pastors disappear in the blink of an eye, tripped up by financial, emotional, or sexual temptations. I've been in a pulpit preaching on a Sunday morning a few days after the former pastor was arrested and hauled off for various sins and crimes.

So, which kind of transition is more difficult to navigate: the long slow death or the sudden disappearance?

It all depends. If the body—the local congregation—is healthy, the heart transplant has a good chance of success. But if the body is ailing, the chances for a successful transplant decrease. That's why healing comes first.

HEALING THE BODY'S "HOLY TRINITY"

I think in terms of the three main parts of the body that need the Transition Leader's healing ministry.

The Congregation

When believers talk and compare notes on the different churches everyone attends, the discussions often move to comparisons of the leaders who stand before these congregations week after week, ministering the Word of God.

> *Pastors are a major part of a church's identity. That's why I call them the beating heart of the body.*

Pastors are a major part of a church's identity. That's why I call them the beating heart of the body. When that heart changes, all the members feel it in powerful and, sometimes, disturbing ways.

As we will see more fully, the Transition Leader is called to step in and serve as the body's temporary heart valve replacement until a strong and healthy heart can be found to fit into a strong and healthy body.

The Staff

The men and women who make churches run are often hit harder and deeper when there's a heart transplant. They're also often the most anxious about what's next, fearful that their jobs may be on the line under the next administration.

When the leader leaves, staff is stretched and tested in new and potentially destructive ways. That's why the Transition Leader needs to surround these junior shepherds with love, prayer, guidance, and support.

Elders and/or Board

If the congregation and staff are being cared for, the body's leadership can roll up its sleeves, get down on its knees, and get to work finding the next shepherd God is calling to serve this body.

Experience shows that few, if any, of these committed servants have ever been through a church leader transition before. But this isn't the Transition Leader's first rodeo. Now it's time to put that experience to work.

CALLING VS. ASSIGNMENT: A PERSONAL REFLECTION

Transitions can be tough on outgoing pastors. Many feel lost without their flock.

The best transitions happen when pastors understand the difference between calling and assignment. Pastors are called by God into ministry, which may be a lifetime calling. But pastoral assignments happen for only a season and only in one place. These are temporary assignments within a lifelong calling to ministry.

Calling doesn't change, but assignments may vary over a lifetime, so it's important to remember that assignments are temporal and will come and go. When a pastor is finished at one church, it doesn't mean that the pastoral calling is over. It's just the end of the current assignment. God still has another assignment for you.

That's the story of my life. I had to let go of one assignment, so I could embrace the next one. I confused my assignment with my calling and hung on to it like it was my baby. Only when I let that assignment go could I see God's next step in His plan for my calling.

PUTTING IT ALL TOGETHER

So far, in this book, I've shown how my experience has led me to my second life calling as a Transition Leader. I've been so grateful that I could serve as a guide, helping navigate churches through the difficulties and challenges that threaten the success of any pastor change.

Now let's take a close look at the proven process you can use to make sure your congregation's next heart transplant is successful.

A Checklist for Change: 47 Ways to Improve Pastoral Transitions

In the next section, I will lead you step-by-step through the five major areas your church will need to address as it navigates the transition process.

Meanwhile, here's a checklist leaders can use to prepare themselves and their flocks for the journey ahead. The following is an excerpt from "50 Ways to Improve Pastoral Transitions," published by the Lewis Center for Church Leadership:[23]

CONCLUDING MINISTRY IN ONE SETTING

Maintain good successor relations
1) Work with the congregation to prepare the way for your successor.
2) Work with your successor to provide good information about the congregation.
3) Spend significant time with your successor with an agreed-upon agenda.
4) Talk about your successor only in positive terms.
5) Avoid making comparisons between yourself and your successor.

---

23 "50 Ways to Improve Pastoral Transitions," *Lewis Center for Church Leadership*, 22 Mar. 2019, https://www.churchleadership.com/50-ways/50-ways-to-improve-pastoral-transitions-2/.

Approach the move with a generous and graceful spirit

1) Share ownership for the move, and avoid blaming others.
2) Avoid making inappropriate use of closure to address unresolved problems.
3) Be gracious to everyone, especially those with whom you have had difficulty.

Provide good records and administrative wrap-up

1) Prepare essential lists for your successor, and be sure important files are up to date.
2) Make sure church bills are paid through the month you leave.
3) Ensure that denominational giving is up to date.
4) Never leave any unpaid personal bills in the community.
5) Do not take church records with you.

Plan for appropriate goodbyes, grief, and closure rituals

1) Provide adequate rituals to mark your leaving and the coming of your successor.
2) Find appropriate ways to say goodbye and grieve with the congregation.
3) Encourage loved ones to grieve the transition, and grieve with them.
4) Grant and ask for forgiveness where needed, and tell the people you love them.

5) Arrange personal visits and write personal notes where appropriate.

Clarify your new relationship with the church
1) Clarify in spoken and written communication your new relationship with the people.
2) Be clear that you will not be returning for pastoral roles.
3) Take time to teach the congregation about closure and boundaries.
4) Affirm love and friendship while releasing persons from pastoral relationships.

Keep working
1) Continue vital ministry, avoid emotional withdrawal, and do not initiate major new programs in the closing months.
2) Settle as many hanging difficulties as possible, including (and especially) staff difficulties.

BEGINNING MINISTRY IN A NEW SETTING

Learn about the new church and community
1) Allow 6–18 months to get to know the people and community.
2) Demonstrate willingness, and make the effort, to learn the history of the congregation.
3) Learn the mission and vision of the congregation and their place in the life of the people.

4) Study data (worship and financial statistics, community demographics, etc.) to understand the church and community.
5) Make careful assessments of strengths, weaknesses, challenges, and opportunities.

Spend time with people and build relationships
1) Make building relationships your highest priority, visiting as many people as you can.
2) Visit people with pastoral needs and also those with key leadership responsibilities.
3) Ask everyone you visit to suggest others with whom you should be talking.
4) Pay particular attention to pastoral care and preaching.
5) Meet community leaders including other clergy. Be visible in the community.
6) Develop a plan to get to know the people, communicate that plan, and stay faithful to it.

Be cautious about making immediate changes
1) Do not change things at first, especially worship.
2) Listen and observe with an open mind to discover strengths and needs.
3) Earn the right to change things before initiating changes.

Build trust
1) Express joy in being in your new ministry setting.

2) Be authentic, honest, and genuine.
3) Let people get to know you, and allow the congregation time to learn to trust you.
4) Focus on the congregation and its future, not your agenda.

Honor your predecessor's ministry
1) Do not criticize the former pastor, even if criticism is warranted.
2) Honor the progress and achievements accomplished before you arrived.
3) Assure people it is all right to grieve the loss of their former pastor.
4) Honor traditions long enough to understand the positive motivation behind them.
5) Throughout it all, keep in mind: Avoid talking about your previous congregation. Do not complain, criticize, or make excessive demands. And be patient.

PART 3
NAVIGATING THROUGH TRANSITION

CHAPTER 8
Embarking on the Transition Journey

When a church faces a transition in pastoral leadership, there are often those in the congregation or even in church leadership who proclaim that such transitions can be handled in a few short weeks, similar to hiring decisions made at small businesses.

"We do this all the time," they say. "It's easy, and it can happen fairly quickly. The last thing we want to do as a church is drag this thing out for months and months."

In reality, pastoral transitions require significant commitments of attention, time, and resources that some members will criticize as overblown.

> *I try to help believers see that navigating a transition is like taking a journey. You can't just hop in the car and start driving with no destination in mind.*

I try to help believers see that navigating a transition is like taking a journey. You can't just hop in the car and start driving with no destination in mind.

In this journey, it may take a while to get where you want to go. The journey may take more time than you expect, and it will probably include more than its share of winding roads—not because people get lost but because, in complex human systems, there is often more going on under the surface than meets the eye.

Leadership transitions affect every part of a church, and the Transition Leader must use a lifetime of experience to guide the flock safely home. I will lead you every step of the way in the five chapters that make up this section of the book.

It's time for our preboarding announcement. Here's a brief checklist covering everything we'll be seeing as we navigate the transition journey.

1: Minister to Congregation

2: Ministry to Church Board & Staff

3: Congregational Assessment

4: Leading the Search Committee

5: Leading the Search Process

6: Post-Transition

PULPIT MINISTRY TO THE CONGREGATION
- Bring spiritual direction to the church.
- Prepare the congregation for the future.
- Cast interim vision plan.
- Develop outward focus.

LEADERSHIP MINISTRY TO CHURCH BOARD, STAFF, ETC.
- Deal with staff issues.
- Provide staff training.
- Strengthen administrative processes and systems.
- Secure alignment for future pastors.

CONGREGATIONAL ASSESSMENT
- Conduct, analyze, and report on full church assessment.
- Determine challenges from the past.
- Articulate core values.
- Deal with critical issues the church will face moving forward.
- Evaluate constitution/bylaws.

LEADING THE SEARCH COMMITTEE
- Assess the church's DNA, using input from assessment.
- Develop present leaders.
- Train leaders in the search process.
- Create a schedule for search, including site visits.
- Put together financial package for new pastor.

LEADING THE SEARCH PROCESS
- Collect names of potential candidates.

- Create profile of your church for new pastor.
- Create profile of ideal pastoral candidate.
- Narrow the list through online sermons.
- Determine top six candidates.
- Search committee site visits.
- Narrow the list to three names.
- Do personal interviews.
- Present selected candidate to church.
- Organize election weekend events.

POST-TRANSITION

- Coach new pastor for six months.
- Help pastor with first-year vision/objectives implementation.
- Pulpit ministry development for six months.

It can be a long journey, but if you're patient and hardworking, it will be more than worth it. Let's break down the entire journey into its component steps and see how you can successfully navigate each one.

CHAPTER 9
Preaching the Flock Through the Transition

Preaching is an important calling, as Paul told Timothy in his second letter to the young leader:

In the presence of God and of Christ Jesus, who will judge the living and the dead, and in view of his appearing and his kingdom, I give you this charge: Preach the word; be prepared in season and out of season; correct, rebuke and encourage—with great patience and careful instruction. —2 Timothy 4:1-2

The calling of the Transition Leader has similarities to Paul's description but with a slightly different emphasis. The Transition Leader's pulpit ministry focuses on the following:

- Spiritually preparing the congregation for their new shepherd.
- Promoting acceptance of change and expressions of grief.
- Bringing the congregation to a place of unity over their identity and needs.
- Giving them the one-year vision plan for navigating the transition.

› Focusing them outward, continuing community service projects and marketplace evangelism initiatives.

A CRUCIAL SEASON

The transition period between the previous pastor and the next pastor is a crucial season in the life of any church, and the Transition Leader must preach the flock through this potentially trying time with more than flowery words or inspirational slogans.

> *The transition period between the previous pastor and the next pastor is a crucial season in the life of any church, and the Transition Leader must preach the flock through this potentially trying time with more than flowery words or inspirational slogans.*

When the flock is without its past shepherd, some sheep may grow fearful or anxious. Others are impatient. They want action now on getting a new pastor, and any delay will only frustrate them more.

In normal times, sound biblical preaching and teaching are the top priorities. But transition time isn't normal time. Members of the flock have different needs during this unusual season. In addition to sound preaching and teaching, you need to bring healing to these sheep.

Sometimes, I imagine what Paul might say to Timothy if Timothy were serving as a Transition Leader. I think his counsel might go something like this: "This is Christ's church, part of His living body. You are called to lead this church only for a season, but for God's sake, make sure you don't let anything harm it or weaken it."

For the Transition Leader, the assignments are simple and straightforward:
› Bring spiritual peace and direction to the church.
› Cast an interim vision plan.
› Prepare the congregation for the future.
› Help the church develop an outward focus.

Let's explore each of these assignments.

BRINGING PEACE AND DIRECTION

You're stopped at a red light at a busy intersection on a rainy night when the power suddenly goes out. In an instant, traffic that was busy but orderly turns into a disordered mess. Some drivers speed through the intersection. Others wait. Others honk their horns.

This is how it feels for some believers living through a pastoral transition. The traffic cop who used to keep things moving along smoothly is gone, and people don't know what to do. Your mission is to calm the chaos by bringing a sense of purpose and direction.

The church may be known for its outreach, service, youth programs, or music, and if the church is healthy, it can continue in all these activities. But there's one difference. During this unique transition season, the church must embrace a new and important mission: surviving the transition and making itself a stronger and more vibrant church than it was before.

The Transition Leader knows this is not the season to launch ambitious new programs or building campaigns. The new pastor can take care of those things when appropriate.

Now is the time to keep things stable and steady by building on the past while also helping people look forward to a new tomorrow.

When I'm helping a church transition, I sometimes start with a sermon series on the fruits of the Spirit because these spiritual characteristics are so important during the transition season.

CASTING A TRANSITION VISION PLAN

How long is this transition going to last? How are things going to work? Who will make all the decisions the pastor used to make?

The members of your search committee may already know the answers to these questions, but few in the congregation have a clue about what's going on unless you make sure you keep them in the loop as part of your Sunday pulpit ministry. Depending on the DNA of the congregation, some will probably want to know nearly every detail while others are perfectly fine entrusting all the messy details to the transition team.

That doesn't mean you need to walk them through the entire transition process on your first Sunday in the pulpit. Instead, I find it best to highlight different parts of the process during successive Sundays, keeping everyone informed of new developments without repeating yourself week after week.

It's also helpful to have members of the search committee explain the process to the congregation. This isn't the Transition Leader's transition. It's the church's transition, and the church needs to own it and understand it. Regular congregational meetings and question-and-answer periods might also be helpful in keeping members apprised and relieving their anxieties.

How much do members need to know about the details of the process? Opinions vary on this.

Jason Lowe, a Southern Baptist pastor and leader who has helped churches through the transition process, believes that too many congregations are left in the dark about what the process involves, leading to unnecessary frustration, suspicion, and conflict.

He has written a helpful and encouraging book for congregations called *The Church During the Search: Honoring Christ While You Wait for Your Next Pastor*.[24] Thankfully, the book is presented in group study format, making it easier to lead church members or even members of your search committee, through the ins and outs of transition.

---

24 Jason Lowe, *The Church During the Search: Honoring Christ While You Wait for Your Next Pastor* (Abbotsford, WI: Aneko Press, 2021).

PREPARING THE CONGREGATION FOR THE FUTURE

Church members know what the past looked like, and they're starting to get a better idea about how the transition process will go. But that still leaves one blank unfilled. What's our future as a church?

No one knows exactly what the future holds, but I try to envision a future for a congregation that is brighter than its past.

> *No one knows exactly what the future holds but I try to envision a future for a congregation that is brighter than its past.*

If the previous pastor was much beloved, the challenge might be persuading them to trust that another pastor can, with God's help, rise to the occasion. If the previous pastor left under a cloud, the challenge may be believing that God can resurrect them and use them once again.

I encourage churches to be prayerful rather than expectant about what tomorrow brings. "Trust God, and pray for your new pastor," I tell them. "God's not through with this church yet. He has much He wants to accomplish for the kingdom through us. Our job now is to prepare ourselves and our church in anticipation of all the blessings and opportunities God promises to bring our way."

HELPING THE CHURCH DEVELOP AN OUTWARD FOCUS

When a pastor leaves and a church enters a time of transition, it's understandable that a church will become—at least somewhat—inward-focused. The Transition Leader's assignment is to help the church be inward-focused for a season, not to develop self-centeredness as a lifelong commitment.

Transitions are important and require churches to take care of complicated business. But the goal of this whole process is a healthy, vibrant, thriving church that not only serves those within its walls but carries Christ's love and message to the broader community.

Paul urged Timothy to be prepared in season and out of season. Likewise, the successful Transition Leader helps the congregation do the necessary inner work and self-assessment required for a successful handoff to the next leader. But he lets them know that once this essential inner work is done, their goal is to get back to being the kind of church that looks beyond its own issues and seeks to meet the needs of the world.

GIVING CHRIST'S SHEEP THE NOURISHMENT THEY NEED

Pulpit ministry is an essential part of the Transition Leader's assignment. During a season of transition, messages that provide hope, healing, purpose, and guidance can ease anxieties and pave the way for the success of the congregation's next leader.

> ### A Management Consultant Takes On Pastoral Transition
>
> William Bridges is a business consultant and the author of *Managing Transitions*.[25] He says people don't resist change, but they do resist transition.
> › Change is situational. People negotiate such outcomes without much trauma.
> › "Transition is the psychological process people go through to come to terms with the loss of the old. Transition begins with ending, and this is where people struggle."
>
> Church consultant Susan Beaumont summarized Bridges's suggestions for making transition easier in her article "Letting Go of This Pastor and Preparing for the Next":[26]
>
> **1) Define what is ending and what is not**
> *When faced with a leadership loss, people often have one of two extreme responses: they pretend that nothing is changing, or they overly dramatize that everything is ending. Helpful leaders invite people to explore what is actually coming to an end and what is not. Talking openly about losses and gains allows everyone to approach the transition with sympathy for those who are feeling the loss more sharply.*

---

25 William Bridges and Susan Bridges, *Managing Transitions: Making the Most of Change* (Lebanon, IN: Da Capo Press, 2017).
26 Susan Beaumont, "Letting Go of This Pastor and Preparing for the Next," *Lewis Center for Church Leadership*, 24 Apr. 2019, https://www.churchleadership.com/leading-ideas/letting-go-of-this-pastor-and-preparing-for-the-next/. =

2) Communicate, communicate, communicate

Overreaction is normal in a transition process. The present loss may trigger previously unresolved losses. Some may perceive this loss as the first of many larger losses to come. Loss often triggers feelings of powerlessness. Powerlessness is mitigated by giving people information. Leaders often assume that people are informed if information has been shared once. In times of anxiety and disorientation, people need to be told again and again. Find as many ways to communicate information as you can: in writing, from the pulpit, in small- and large-group gatherings. Don't assume that since the leaders know, the rank and file know too.

Don't confuse confidentiality with secret-keeping. Some stages of pastoral transition require confidentiality. We can't reveal the identity of possible candidates during a search and call process. However, we don't have to keep secrets about where we are in the process, who is making decisions on our behalf, what practices we are using, or which leadership attributes we value. Talk about these things as much as possible.

Don't wait for all the details to become available. Share what you know. You may be inclined to wait for everything to be perfectly clear before you begin communicating. Start the communication process as soon as you have something to share. Be straightforward about what is known and what is yet unclear, at every stage of the transition.

3) Tell the story

A good ending narrative respects the past but does not get stuck there. It helps people see that a good ending helps ensure the continuity of what is most important to them.

It creates the opportunity for an honest accounting of both triumphs and failures, and it wards off false idealization of the past. It avoids selective memory. It helps people realize that this chapter has to end in order for tomorrow's changes to materialize. By addressing loss forthrightly, congregations make emotional space for new beginnings and attachments.

When Moses stood at the edge of the promised land, knowing that he would not go further, he chose that moment to retell his people's story. By remembering their past experiences, he helped them recognize God's faithfulness at other times when they experienced transition and went on to create new meanings in the future. We can do the same by helping congregations learn that times of loss, experienced openly and fully, lead into times of promise.

CHAPTER 10
Leading the Leaders

After Christ's church was born on the Day of Pentecost, leaders were installed to shepherd the flock: "Paul and Barnabas appointed elders for them in each church and, with prayer and fasting, committed them to the Lord, in whom they had put their trust" (Acts 14:22-24).

Paul later provided additional guidance for elders and other leaders: "The elders who direct the affairs of the church well are worthy of double honor, especially those whose work is preaching and teaching" (1 Timothy 5:12).

Church leaders play an important role in the life of a church, and they must come together to help their congregation if a transition is to be successful. The Transition Leader needs to minister to and lead these leaders throughout the entire transition process. If that doesn't happen, things can quickly go off track.

But in many cases, church leaders have emotional issues around change that must be heard and addressed. In some cases, leaders have been traumatized by a pastor's sudden exit or pattern of misbehavior. Let's look at one of those cases.

BETTER LATE THAN NEVER

Pretty much everyone at a church in New Jersey I worked with knew something was fishy about how the pastor had operated things during his long tenure there.

Even worse, they knew that after forty years in the pulpit, their ninety-year-old pastor had to go sooner or later, but he seemed to be hanging on for dear life. Finally, the pastor made a decision that forced him out. Not only had the pastor stayed too long and tried to carry on long after his effectiveness was gone, but he had also created a personality cult around himself that provided cover for decades of greed.

When I was first contacted to help this church transition to its next leader, I had no idea about the mess I was walking into. Soon enough, I found myself in a toxic environment that, once the pastor was gone, had no real functioning organization. He had removed all real checks and balances. The church had the normal constitution or bylaws, but these hadn't been followed.

I knew what my mission must be. I would need to bring healing to this troubling environment and remove the sickness that had allowed so much to go wrong. I also knew that I would be spending much of my time working to change the DNA of the church's leadership and forming a new group of church leaders who would be selected by church members.

WHY DO THEY STAY?

In some cases, frightened and abused members of churches remind me of women who remain in abusive relationships. In either case, I ask myself, *Why do they stay?*

I'm not a psychologist or a police officer, but I've heard some women's stories about the horrible abuse they endure. I hurt for victims who try to conceal bruises and scars in an effort to protect their assailants.

As best I can understand, some stay in abusive situations because they've been programmed to believe that they are bad people who don't deserve anything better. Some stay out of fear, afraid they will experience worse abuse should they leave. Some assume that their current situation, no matter how bad, is better than any alternatives they know of.

The psychology seems similar in churches where powerful leaders assume the role of an abusive spiritual father.

If you find yourself helping guide a transition from an abusive leader, don't try to move ahead without understanding and addressing the emotional dimensions of the abuse on church members, leaders, and staff. In the case of the New Jersey church, we made counseling available to the many people who had suffered abuse and emotional harm.

Long story short, after 2.5 years of work, the church elected a new pastor. The transition went well, and he continues to effectively lead the congregation several years later.

Every time there is a transition, the Transition Leader needs to clean up old issues before new issues can be addressed. In some cases, these old issues are so significant that extensive surgery is needed to remove diseased tissue and prepare this congregation for the next step in its future.

FILLING THE VACUUM

Before His crucifixion, Jesus predicted His death, citing the prophet Zechariah: "I will strike the shepherd, and the sheep of the flock will be scattered" (Zechariah 13:7).

I've seen many cases where the sudden disappearance of a pastor led to sheep being scattered amid chaos and confusion. More often than not, church leaders—both elders and board members—often try to fill that vacuum themselves. The scenario often plays out like this:

> - The leader leaves, and to fill the vacuum, the board tries to run things.
> - The staff sees gaps and omissions in what the board is doing and tries to fill in these gaps itself.
> - Finally, congregation members see gaps and omissions in what the board and the staff are doing and fearlessly try to fill the vacuum themselves.

The result is chaos because when everyone is in charge, nobody is in charge. In the absence of a shepherd, the sheep go into overdrive but in different directions.

WHAT LEADERS NEED

Whether a transition is smooth or chaotic, the Transition Leader is ministering to more than just the members of the congregation. Church leaders need healing and guidance too. Here are six specific needs the Transition Leader must address:

1) Deal With Staff Issues

Every workplace has issues that need to be addressed, including churches. If the previous pastor has left everything in a mess, the Transition Leader may be forced to deal with more issues. Even in a church that has been managed well, some leaders may harbor hurts, fears, anxieties, or trauma from their experiences.

Some of these issues may be hard to detect, but pay attention to what needs to be done, and act on it. The answer is not ignoring or papering over staff issues. Doing this only starts a ticking time bomb that may go off once the new leader arrives.

2) Work on Process and Systems

President Harry S. Truman had a sign on his desk that read: "The Buck Stops Here." That might be a great motto for a president, but it's not always the best approach for a pastor. If a church is transitioning from a pastor who insisted that every buck stopped with him, the Transition Leader will need to create a system that enables the church's business and staffing functions to be run effectively, no matter who the pastor is.

3) Staff Training

Church employees play an essential role in the life of a church, but many do so blindly, without the preparation and training that can help them not only succeed but even exceed expectations. The Transition Leader must connect with staff, hear their hearts as well as hear about their problems, help them, heal what can be healed, and prepare people to fulfill the calling they have received.

4) Alignment for Future Pastor

Before a church is ready for a new leader, some homework must be done and some hard questions must be asked. In the next chapter, we will talk about assessment which is an essential step on the road to a successful transition. As the congregation is going through its assessment process, church leaders and staff need to go through a similar process that presents the incoming leader with a united board and staff, not a conflict zone with warring parties.

5) Put Together a Financial Package for the New Pastor

Another upcoming chapter deals with the pastoral search process. That process will turn out much better if church leadership constructs a generous but realistic financial package for the new pastor. Some churches try to get by with a bare-bones budget, but this may prove unattractive to potential candidates. No church wants to break the bank, but pastors are to be treated with honor and compensated appropriately for their essential work.

If the outgoing pastor plans to stay on until his successor starts, the church should also provide an honorable financial farewell that will help them pursue future endeavors and release their position for the better of the church.

Also keep in mind the new pastor's expenses for moving and questions about whether the pastor's spouse will be performing valuable functions that should also be compensated.

6) Train Leaders in the Search Process

Eventually, you will be creating a search committee that takes the lead on the pastoral search process, but other leaders have important roles they must perform too. The Translation Leader needs to prepare everyone in leadership and staff positions for the complicated and time-consuming process they're about to start.

There are a number of good resources that can be used in training the search committee members and other church leaders. Pastor Chris Brauns of Illinois has written a book that many churches have found helpful. *When the Word Leads Your Pastoral Search: Biblical Principles & Practices to Guide Your Search* is a solid study that you can use with members of your search committee and others closely involved in the process. Brauns says a successful search "must focus on God's Word and how the candidate relates to it and preaches from it."[27]

This kind of approach can help people apply biblical principles to the process and not rely solely on personality or pulpit skills.

BOARD RESPONSIBILITIES AND PRINCIPLES

I always try to make sure that church boards follow these principles when working their way through a transition.

---

[27] Chris Brauns, *When the Word Leads Your Pastoral Search: Biblical Principles and Practices to Guide Your Search* (Chicago, IL: Moody Publishers, 2011).

1) Confidentiality

It is of utmost importance that all members of the board keep all information about the search for a new pastor confidential until the board and search committee agree the information should be released. We will help define a timeline of who should know what and by when, and it is essential to keep the congregation informed about the process. Until then, loose lips can sink ships. Ill-timed dissemination of information can be perilous to the entire process.

2) Agreement on process

The board will need to agree on the plan and process before its implementation. If there is disagreement and division here, it will only hinder the process later on.

3) Following the guidance of constitution and bylaws

Most churches do not address succession and transition in their constitution and bylaws. If it is covered there, the guidelines are probably outdated and need to be amended. If there are no guidelines, an amendment is also necessary to add them.

4) Open conversations

Open, honest, and transparent dialogue will facilitate a healthy environment for the board to engage in the transition process. In situations that have lacked openness in the past, a commitment to openness now can be a real blessing to members and the entire congregation, as I saw demonstrated at one board meeting.

A NEW BEGINNING

I was in my sixth week helping the leaders at the Christian Life Center when an amazing transformation happened.

It had been a year since the previous pastor left the church without real spiritual leadership, creating a vacuum that everyone tried to fill. Staff tried to lead. The board tried to lead. Members of the congregation tried to lead. With everybody in charge, nobody was in charge. Many found the chaos uncomfortable. Suddenly, at one of our board meetings, a woman who was involved in the search committee made a startling confession.

"Ron, I want to thank you because, for first time in years, I feel safe at church again."

This was a powerful revelation. The woman had never before confessed that she felt unsafe at the church, but now that we were bringing healing and stability to a chaotic situation, she and others around the table were beginning to feel better. This allowed them to bring things to the surface that had troubled them in the past. And once we had dealt with this baggage, the load was lightened on the rest of our journey.

It's no fun airing dirty laundry, but it's a great thing when you can get dirty laundry clean and make it fresh and usable once again.

Leading the leaders is one of the Transition Leader's key roles. The work can be slow and painful, but when it's completed, the prospects for the new pastor already look better. And in this case, the transition succeeded.

RECOMMENDED SPIRITUAL GROWTH RESOURCES FOR YOUR BOARD/STAFF

When I help lead church leaders through a transition, the pastor in me wants to see them grow spiritually through this process. I realize that many of these people work full-time elsewhere and volunteer their services to the church. I don't want to overburden them during an already challenging season. But some are paid by the church and can do assignments as part of their work.

Either way, spend at least part of your time with the team, building them up spiritually and helping them become wiser and better leaders for the church. I turn to these resources time and again:

- Spiritual Leadership by J. Oswald Sanders
- The Go-Giver by Bob Burg & John David Mann
- Cracking Your Church's Culture Code by Samuel R. Chand
- Developing the Leader Within You by John C. Maxwell
- Developing the Leaders Around You by John C. Maxwell
- The Five Levels of Leadership by John C. Maxwell

22 Transition Mistakes to Avoid

Jimmy Dodd is a former pastor and the founder of Pastor Serve, a ministry to pastors. He is also the author of two books for leaders: *Survive or Thrive* and *Pastors are People Too*. I've adapted his list of "The 22 Most Common Mistakes Made by

Church Leadership Teams During a Time of Senior Pastor Transition."[28]

1) Neglecting Prayer as a Priority
Hit the pause button. Take a deep breath, fall on your knees, and humbly seek the face of God.

2) Failure to take a Holistic Approach – Piecing a Transition Plan together
A church in transition must have a unified cohesive plan.

3) Failure to Engage with Church Health Best Practices
A church must address complacency, apathy, and ignorance in regards to missing essential elements of the church. Address that which has been neglected.

4) Failure to Appoint an Interim Leader/Pastor
An interim leader provides the congregation with a sense of stability, consistency, and peace.

5) Refusal to Seek Outside Help. Operating in a Vacuum
Outside consultants provide valuable insight. Denominational or network affiliations can be extremely valuable.

6) Trying to "business our way out of this mess"
Must humbly look to the leading/guidance of the Holy Spirit.

---

[28] Jimmy Dodd, "The 22 Most Common Mistakes Made by Leadership Teams During a Time of Senior Pastor Transition," *PastorServe*, 10 Mar. 2020, https://pastorserve.org/common-mistakes-of-pastor-transitions/.

7) Ignoring weighty past issues with the mindset of "Today is a new day. It's time to bury the past and look forward"
This neglects the need to process, heal, and grieve.

8) Failure to tell the truth. No truth = No Trust
Recovery is nearly impossible when church members perceive they were deceived.

9) Manage Sin
Covering sin, hiding sin, and spinning sin will ultimately destroy a church.

10) Not counting the cost – both financially and personally.
Giving will likely drop in the short term. Delegation is essential as no one person or group can bear the burden alone.

11) When a pastor leaves amid dissatisfaction with his or her performance, during the search process, swinging the pastor pendulum to the opposite side.
Far too many churches over-compensate for the weakness of the previous pastor by looking for pastoral personalities that are opposite to the departed pastor.

12) No Clear Plan for Congregational Communication – Lack of Communication
Staff and congregation must be kept in the loop by the elders and the search committee. Regular updates are essential.

13) Failure of the Elders and Staff to Rise to an Appropriate Transition Leadership Level

A pastoral transition will result in everyone needing to "step up their game." This is a season—which must be recognized once the work is done.

14) *Failure to Celebrate!!*
Celebrate a job well done. Many will give sacrificially during a pastoral transition. Honor these people for their work.

CHAPTER 11
Assess to Bless

Assessing the current health and vitality of a church is an essential step in every leadership transition. What are a church's strengths and weaknesses? What does it do well, and where does it stumble?

When churches don't monitor themselves, they can find the outside world willing to weigh in on their sins. That was the case with one church that made the local news—and not in the way they wanted.

GHOSTS IN THE CLOSET

I don't even want to mention the name of the worst church situation I've ever seen. I could write an entire book on the problems this church faced. These brief highlights (or low lights) should suffice. At this church:

› An aged and authoritarian pastor stayed way too long, turning a church into his own political and financial kingdom.
› Cult-like tendencies emerged.
› The church owned a forest overseas.

> The church also owned and paid insurance on thirty-two automobiles, some of which were lent to church members.

However, what really got this pastor in trouble was his greed and the unique—some would say evil—methods he used to generate money.

After everything blew up, I began working with the church to turn things around. I sat down and met with the church board. That night they told me that I was the first outsider who had been allowed into one of their meetings in more than thirty years.

WHO AM I? WHO ARE WE?

During adolescence, many young people ask themselves questions like, "Who am I?" and "What do I want to do with my life?" Churches need to ask and answer these kinds of questions when they go through a transition process. The need is even greater when a congregation is trying to right itself after an unhealthy period.

Jesus cares about the health of the churches that make up His body. As He warned the church of Laodicea: "I know your deeds, that you are neither cold nor hot. I wish you were either one or the other! So, because you are lukewarm—neither hot nor cold—I am about to spit you out of my mouth" (Revelation 3:15-16).

We should care too. That's why churches need to ask themselves, "Who are we?" and "How are we supposed to serve Christ?"

Asking and answering these questions are what churches do during an assessment. It is a crucial stage in any successful transition.

FOUR QUESTIONS CHURCHES MUST ANSWER

There are four key questions that a church should consider as they formulate a transition plan. If the outgoing pastor is still part of the church, he can assist in this process. If not, church leaders must help their church figure out who they are.

I have provided assessment forms your church can use in the final section of this book. Before you look at those materials, briefly consider the four key questions an assessment must answer.

Question 1: Where are we?

Start by taking an environmental audit of the four key areas of church life:

> Where are we spiritually today in our church?
> Where are we relationally today in our church?
> Where are we financially today in our church?
> What are our core values?

Different members may have varied answers to these first two questions. As for the third question, there may be many members that have no clue about the church's financial health. The church's financial team can help bring them up to speed on money matters.

Examples of Core Values

What's a core value? Many people struggle with this simple question. I don't want to box your church in but provide you with some value statements your team can use to start the discussion. Don't copy these. Instead, come up with original statements that articulate your church's values.

Example 1: We Passionately Pursue Jesus.
> We keep the main thing the main thing. People are transformed by God through His holy and perfect Word, the Bible, prayer, and worship.

Example 2: We Fully Embrace the Power of the Holy Spirit.
> We acknowledge the Holy Spirit and His work in everything we do. He is there to lead, guide, and help us through every part of every day.

Example 3: We Encourage People to Ongoing Improvement.
> We encourage people to take the NEXT STEP to discover their God-given potential. Our church is a joyous place where we can grow in knowledge, love, and contentment.

Example 4: We Create Opportunities for Every Person to Use Their Gifts.
> We share our talents, passions, time, and gifts to serve others. We believe prayer and creativity are keys to fulfilling our vision.

Example 5: We Are a Family Who Is Better Together.
> We are a multicultural, multiethnic family united under one God-given vision. We pray for one another and extend grace to one another.

Example 6: We Live to Give.
> We are contributors, not consumers. We lead the way in generosity. No amount of money, resources, or effort

is insignificant in our attempts to reach those in need of Jesus.

Example 7: We Invest in the Next Generation.
› We train, equip, and commission the next generation. We pray for and partner with parents to help them raise children who love God and serve others.

Example 8: We Act in Audacious Faith.
› We act in faith to set impossible goals, take bold steps, and watch God move. In order to fulfill our vision, we think big with an outward focus on others.

Question 2: Where do we want to go?

Question one was about where we are today. This second question is about where we want to be tomorrow as a congregation. Everyone needs to do a bit of forecasting and paint the picture of where they would like the church to be between five and ten years from now.

Question 3: What or who is in our way?

What is it about our church today that keeps us from becoming the church we envision for tomorrow? The goal of this question is to discover the foreseeable obstacles we need to address to fulfill our calling as a congregation. Once a church figures out if there are challenges from the past that are keeping it from being what it needs to be today, it can figure out what it needs to be tomorrow.

Question 4: How do we get there?

We figured out what the obstacles are. Once these are out of our way, what steps do we need to take, and what changes do we need to institute to move forward and get closer to where we want to be? Then, define a strategy and tactics to move in the right direction.

Everyone in the congregation needs to answer these questions, and everyone's questions need to be heard and addressed.

Church leadership has one additional question it needs to answer: Are our church constitution and bylaws up-to-date and sufficient to meet the challenges the church faces today? Oftentimes, these documents were labored over decades ago, filed away, and never consulted again. Transition time is the perfect time to dust off the church's official documents, evaluate them, and update them as needed as the church journeys through the transition process.

Sample Assessment Questions
A good assessment depends on good questions. If you ask weak questions, you will get weak answers. Instead of bland generalities, seek specific comments that identify particular strengths or weaknesses.

Sample 1: What is the unique or distinctive characteristic that distinguishes this congregation from the other churches in the community?

Sample 2: What do you see as the most pressing issue or concern on the congregation's current agenda?

Sample 3: What do you believe is the number one asset here? Brag about this congregation.

Sample 4: What is the weakest area of ministry here?

Sample 5: Why would a new guest come here for the first time? Why would they come back?

TIPS FOR A SUCCESSFUL ASSESSMENT

Grace Ruiter's "Pastoral Transition Survival Guide" says, "A pastoral transition is a great time to take stock of your church's current reality; in fact, this should be an essential step in your pastoral search.

It recommends:

Take time to examine your church's current ministry before you actively seek out any pastoral candidates. Survey church members, and examine their feedback carefully. Consider seeking input from the community around your church as well.

Taking the time for a survey process offers your church an opportunity to examine itself: to learn what it has become, what its gifts are, who its people are and what their gifts are, what the community is like and how it's changing, and, most importantly, what your church might be doing next in ministry.[29]

How to Gather Feedback or Conduct a Survey

Decide how you, as a pastoral search team, want to gather feedback on your church. Keep in mind that you can use more than one method to collect information. Compile a set of questions you can ask that gets to the heart of your church's ministry.

This time of congregational feedback allows you to involve many people in the process—not just the search

---

29 Grace Ruiter, "Pastoral Transition Survival Guide: How to Navigate a Pastoral Search and Transition," *Faithward.org*, 18 May 2021, https://www.faithward.org/pastoral-transition-survival-guide-how-to-navigate-a-pastoral-search-and-transition/.

team. The pastoral search team could conduct a survey of the entire congregation with a carefully prepared questionnaire. Various groups (consistory, staff, lay leaders, etc.) should be interviewed for their input. Congregational dinners provide an excellent setting for the search team to get input from church members.

Sharing and Applying Your Findings

Following the survey, the pastoral search team should write a summary that describes what the survey has revealed and includes some goal statements for your congregation. The team should also share this document with potential candidates for the church. They will want to know the results of the congregational feedback and the goals the church has for the future.

Assessing Your Church's Ministry Systems

Unless a church wants to repeatedly recreate the wheel for each and every Sunday service or other event, it adopts systems for its programs and develops the personnel and resources needed to conduct these programs.

What does your church do, and how does it get it done? Your next pastor will want solid answers to these questions. Perform an assessment of your church's many programs, and detail the systems and people involved in successfully executing them week after week.

Use this brief list as a start for your assessment of essential ministry systems:

- Administrative
- Communication
- Financial
- Weekend services
- Discipleship
- Outreach
- Assimilation
- Etc.

MAKING THINGS BETTER

I've seen more than my share of church disasters. I'm not shocked by anything anymore, but I do occasionally get depressed. Thankfully, God has granted me a strong constitution that helps me remain steady in my calling.

There's one other thing that keeps me going. Hope.

Time and time again I've seen how even the most dire of situations can be redeemed and transformed by God's power working through God's people. That's what happened with the New Jersey church in this chapter and with Christian Life Center in the previous chapter.

Christ has unique callings for each church in His body. Leading a church through an in-depth assessment process can help it figure out what's holding it back and prepare it to fulfill its calling as a congregation.

CHAPTER 12

The Church Starts Its Search

There's good news for churches if the Transition Leader has been able to do what we've been talking about in the last three chapters:
- Ministering to the flock.
- Leading the leaders.
- And helping the church assess where it is and where it wants to go.

If these projects are well underway, you can now move on to the one part of the process that people are most interested in seeing succeed: the search for a new pastor.

However, if these processes are not taking place, it can be risky to bring a new leader into this scenario. There are churches that believe they can rush the search process. Belief alone, though, doesn't always generate the desired results.

When a rapid succession doesn't work, the consequences are as sad to see as they are unnecessary.

SHORTCHANGING THE SEARCH

Sometimes an unsuccessful transition happens because a pastor wants to leave but doesn't want to go through the entire process of searching for a successor, particularly when he mistakenly thinks he has the right candidate in mind.

Sometimes it's a church board that initiates an unsuccessful transition after a pastor has left, and they suddenly scramble to fill the pulpit with somebody—or anybody—who can preach a decent sermon.

There might be many reasons a congregation would want to attempt a quick search, but churches that skip these six essential steps are risking the success of their transition:

Step 1: Assess Church's Core Values

Step 2: Use Values to Seek Best Candidates

Step 3: Review Candidates

Step 4: Narrow Candidate List

Step 5: Sermons and Site Visits

Step 6: Recommendation to Church Leadership

We will expand on each of these steps in the following pages. This will be the longest chapter in the book because I have supplied you with resources and tips that can help you succeed.

DISCORD AT CONCORD

The word concord means peace and agreement, but there was little peace at this church outside of Charlotte, North Carolina after their pastor chose a successor who, for various reasons, didn't work out and was eventually not chosen by the congregation. Unfortunately, things often fail to work out when people try to transition without following the principles and plans that you're reading about.

The church was a big assignment, including a church, a Christian school, a shopping center, and a Christian camp. Unfortunately, these administrative and financial responsibilities of the senior pastor's job description proved overwhelming to a chosen successor who was a good preacher and solid leader but simply lacked the experience needed to oversee such an ecclesiastical enterprise.

The congregation tried to go along with the new choice but ultimately, decided not to elect the new candidate. I was soon answering my phone and heard a voice ask, "Ron, can you be in our pulpit Sunday?"

I worked with this church for several months leading their transition. We were able to find Rick Ross, their new pastor, who was elected in a relatively short period of time. The church grew over the next decade as Rick mentored many leaders inside the church, including one young man who went away to work as the state youth director but was called back to serve as Rick's chosen successor. He, too, enjoyed a successful transition and, years later, is still serving as their leader.

BREAK-UP AT BETHEL

Bethel means house of God, but a church in Wichita, Kansas, became a house of chaos and confusion after the long-term pastor suddenly retired without any buffer, interim pastor, or succession plan.

As often happens, the church board rushed in to save the day. They quickly brought in his successor, whom they introduced cold turkey to the congregation without preparing church members for the change.

Unfortunately, the new leader was not even in the ballpark for what this church wanted or needed. The DNA just didn't match. He lasted ten months.

I worked with the congregation for a year and a half to help them find their next pastor. Following the steps I've outlined, we conducted an assessment to get a better handle on the church's identity and the kind of leader they needed. Our candidate clicked, and he remains in place a decade later.

FORMING A SEARCH COMMITTEE

The Transition Leader helps form a search committee, leads the committee in its work, and meets with them regularly as they define their needs and consider candidates.

The job description for the ideal candidates for a search committee looks something like this: "Help wanted. One- to two-year assignment. Some travel necessary. Key requirement: deep commitment to Christ and His body. No pay. Eternal rewards."

That's all true. You are going to need a committed group of people (some say half a dozen; others say a minimum of nine to fifteen people). These loyal servants must be willing to take on this assignment as a major part of their lives and ministries for the foreseeable future. I've seen search committees wrap up their work in a year, but it often takes two.

Your search committee must represent your church. I've seen too many cases where groups of white men try to represent congregations that are at least 50 percent female and not all white. Make sure your committee reflects the gender and racial/ethnic makeup of your congregation.

Once you have your people lined up, familiarize them with the group's long list of assignments.

Qualifications for Your Search Committee Members

What kind of people should sit on your church's search committee? I've found that it is best to limit the group to people who possess these characteristics:

> Committed to church leadership. They are supportive and helpful in season and out.
> Ten years or more of membership at the church. Newer members may not grasp the church's legacy and mission.

- Unbiased and open-minded. Like attorneys seeking a jury, you are seeking people who don't enter the process convinced about what they should do. They are willing to learn along the way.
- Involved in ministry. Hiring a pastor is not the same as hiring a new CEO for a company. People with experience in church or parachurch ministries may provide better guidance to the group.
- Trusted to be confidential. Loose lips sink ships, and search team members who provide selective information to friends along the way can sink your search efforts. Your team will regularly communicate its progress to the congregation, but it doesn't benefit from members who offer their own unapproved news items or opinions about the process.
- People of integrity. Choose people with proven wisdom, vast experience, and sound judgment.
- Age twenty-five and above. Adulthood is a good prerequisite.
- Maturity. More than age, spiritual and emotional maturity can help the team arrive at sound conclusions.
- Spirit-led. Pastoral leadership is a spiritual position. Your church is hiring more than a CEO; it is hiring a shepherd who can shepherd the flock with the Holy Spirit's wisdom, power, and gifting.
- Financial commitment. Whether they are wealthy or of more humble circumstances, they share their resources with the church.

› Representation of the church body. You will want your group to represent the gender, racial, and sociological makeup of your congregation.

Selecting the Right Search Team Chairperson

Your search team needs a strong and dedicated chairperson to guide the search process over the next year or two. The Transition Leader runs the search committee's meetings, but the chairperson leads everything else, so choosing a good chair is important to your success.

Here are key qualifications to consider as you choose your chairperson:
› Highly organized.
› Clear communication skills.
› Strong group facilitation skills.
› Ability to be impartial and let the team do its work.
› Someone who is respected and trusted by the team.

The chairperson will be responsible for the following tasks:
› Schedule the team meetings.
› Plan the agenda.
› Chair group interviews of all potential candidates.
› Articulate the group's consensus.
› Encourage team members in their service.
› Follow up quickly on group decisions.
› Report monthly to the congregation regarding progress of the team's work.

The Search Committee's Nine Assignments

There's more to a search than reviewing resumes and watching sermons. I will provide you with forms you can use during this process in the final section. But first, let's take a quick look at the process you should follow.

1) Collect potential names.

Once word gets out about your church's search, the flood of resumes will begin. You may also receive recommendations from the outgoing pastor, staff, and members who are trying to help out. Graciously receive everything you are given, but don't do anything with it yet, as experience shows that it's unlikely these people will be your next leader.

2) Create a church profile that tells candidates about your congregation.

Remember that congregational assessment you did? Now you have a better handle on who you are as a congregation and what you are called to do. Summarize these insights so that candidates can understand who you are and what you're looking for. Make sure you also include the kinds of important details that any incoming pastor would ask, such as attendance, demographic information, facilities details, annual budget, indebtedness, etc.

3) Create a pastor profile of your ideal candidate.

Now that your congregation knows where it wants to go, it should be relatively easy to describe some of the key characteristics needed in a leader who can help you realize this vision. Are you looking for a CEO or a shepherd? Figure that out in advance, and let your candidates know what you want. You can even send your pastor profile to leaders you know of who might be a good fit, even if they haven't reached out to you.

4) *Narrow the candidate list through online sermons.*

Love it or hate it, our digital world makes some kinds of research a lot easier. Now that you have your pastor profile in place, it will be easy for you to use this guide as a tool for evaluating candidates. When you've come up with a list of ten or twenty candidates you think might work, committee members need to start checking out their sermons online. During COVID-19, even many churches that had never posted services online started doing so. This enables your group to keep its investigative work private, so it doesn't intrude on the lives of candidates you may not even talk to.

5) *Determine the top six candidates.*

Narrow your candidate list based on the sermons everyone heard and other online research you've conducted about the candidates and their congregations.

6) *Conduct search committee site visits.*

Here's where the travel comes in. Hopefully, your entire search committee can coordinate their calendars and pay visits to the churches where your candidates preach. Then meet and process the results of your visits to narrow down your list once again.

7) Narrow the list to three names.

Now it's time to cut your list of six in half based on everyone's feedback from the site visit. No calls should be made to final candidates until the list is narrowed down to three or four names so that we don't interfere in the lives of pastors and their families.

8) Do personal interviews.

Set up times for your committee to do Zoom interviews with each one of your top candidates. Then, compare notes and narrow your list to your final choice. Conduct your vote on the final candidate by secret ballot.

9) Present your selected candidate to the church.

Your committee has been keeping your congregation updated with each new step in this lengthy process. Now it's time for the final step: the grand unveiling of your chosen candidate.

THE CANDIDATE WEEKEND

I don't like to see a candidate face a congregation for the first time from behind a pulpit. I prefer an introduction process that gives people multiple opportunities to engage the candidate at close range. Churches that want transitions to succeed should plan a Candidate Weekend that creates more time and space for good interaction.

A Candidate Weekend should include:
- A Friday evening meet-and-greet where church members can meet the new pastor and his family in an informal social setting.
- A Saturday "town hall" meeting where the new pastor answers questions people submit on 3" x 5" cards.
- Sermon(s) on Sunday morning.
- A congregational vote.

QUALIFICATIONS FOR YOUR NEW PASTOR

What does your church need in its new pastor? Your church profile and pastor profile are a good start, but you need to define your needs more clearly.

Here is a list of 10 Pastor Priorities you may want to consider in your church.

1) Believe and practice the doctrinal statement of the church.
2) At least fifteen years of ministry experience.
3) Successfully pastored a church and/or led a parachurch ministry.
4) Secure person: able to embrace the legacy of the past without making everything about them!
5) Proven leadership ability, both to lead people and lead change in the church.
6) Passion for the lost.
7) Biblical worldview.
8) Pulpit skills: ability to communicate biblical truths effectively and compellingly to multiple generations.

9) Proven track record of effectively growing a ministry that's under his/her leadership.
10) A people person and mentor who develops the strengths of others in the church.

PASTOR PRIORITIES WORKSHEET

Below is a handy document you can use to evaluate your candidates based on the 10 Pastor Priorities above. Search team members should use this worksheet to evaluate the candidates, even more so as you narrow down your lists.

Low--------to---------High

1) Believe and practice the doctrinal statement of the church.
    1 2 3 4 5
2) At least 15 years of ministry experience.
    1 2 3 4 5
3) Led church of 1,000 or a major parachurch ministry.
    1 2 3 4 5
4) Secure person—able to embrace the legacy of the past.
    1 2 3 4 5
5) Ability to lead people effectively and lead change.
    1 2 3 4 5
6) Passion for the lost.
    1 2 3 4 5
7) Biblical worldview.
    1 2 3 4 5
8) Pulpit skills to reach multiple generations.
    1 2 3 4 5

9) Proven experience in growing a ministry.
    1 2 3 4 5
10) Mentor who develops new leaders.
    1 2 3 4 5
Total =

MAKING SURE CANDIDATES MATCH YOUR CHURCH'S VALUES

Much of what a pastor does is public, particularly when it comes to preaching and leadership. But much of what makes a pastor isn't quite so visible, especially when it comes to personal life and values. Make sure you dig beneath the outward surface qualities of the candidates seeking to be your new leader.

I've developed a list of qualifications that can be broken down into four areas:

1) Personal Life
2) Communication Skills
3) Values
4) Demonstrated Leadership

Here, I have fleshed out these qualifications in a bit more detail. Let's take a look at this detailed list:

Personal Life
› Leads family effectively
› Personal ethics.
› Spousal commitment and support
› Integrity
› Reputation in previous ministry
› Exemplary lifestyle

Communication Skills
- Pulpit ministry—expository and biblical
- Relational skills in church and community
- Teaching ministry
- Preach for transformation and decision/change

Values
- Personal growth
- Developer of people
- Spirit-led/Spirit-filled
- Passion for the lost
- Knows his/her spiritual giftings
- Disciplined lifestyle
- Philosophy of city and church
- Worshiper
- Person of prayer—devotional life

Demonstrated Leadership
- Spiritual leadership
- Organizational—working with people and multiple staff
- Time manager
- Ability to lead change and take risks
- Visionary
- Values legacy of past
- Secure person
- Financial skills

Finally, I have turned the above details into a series of questions that your team can ask its candidates.

Personal Life Questions
Balance
1) How do you balance your personal life with your pastoral duties?
2) What do you enjoy doing in your leisure time?

Family/Marriage
1) What extracurricular activities do you maintain with your family?
2) Talk about your family responsibilities combined with your spouse's commitment to and support of your ministry/lifestyle.
3) What are you doing to enrich your marriage?
4) How does your spouse/family feel about the possibility of relocating?
5) What role does your spouse play in your ministry?

Personal
1) How do you facilitate and ensure your personal spiritual growth?
2) Describe your lowest point in life and your highest point in life.

Finances
How do you handle family finances?

Legacy
How do you believe a member of your present church congregation would describe your leadership, personal life, communication, skills, and values?

Public/Private Perception
How should a pastor's life differ from the average person's lifestyle?

Personal Passion
What is your greatest passion?

Accountability
To whom are you accountable? What accountability systems do you have in your life?

Accomplishments
What is your greatest accomplishment in your present church?

Communication Skills Questions

Generational
How do you appeal to all generations in the delivery of your message?

Evangelism
Do you always give the opportunity to make a decision for Christ in your services?

Preaching
Describe your process (or how you decide the objective) for your weekly sermons.

Comment on:
> Selected subject vs. through a whole book from the Bible over a number of weeks
> Old Testament vs. New Testament
> Distribution of sermon notes to the congregation
> How to communicate to our fellowship regarding miracles, blessings, and dedicated ministries by lay persons, etc.

1) Is your preaching style topical, expository, or narrative? What do you consider to be a good balance between them?
2) What is more important to you: that people know the Bible or that the Word transforms them?
3) What are some of your strengths as a preacher?
4) How do you provide growth for your members and also provide an environment that is welcome to new and nonbelievers?
5) Explain your preaching style, including the value and need to share the pulpit with other pastors on staff and with guest speakers?
6) What are your feelings about the team approach to sharing the pulpit?

Creativity/Media

Do you see value in using multimedia in your sermons? How have you used it in the past?

Leadership/Vision

How do you prepare a congregation for change and help them in the process of making the change?

Community
1) How important is your relationship with the community? How important is the church's relationship?
2) What kind of relationships do you have with other pastors or city leaders in your area?
3) Would you say you are a person that other pastors in your community look to?

Values Questions

Growth—Staff & Congregation
1) What do you feel is the ideal path to develop a new believer into an active member of the body of Christ?
2) What denominational meetings or conferences do you attend?
3) What kinds of activities do you do to help you grow as a Christian, family man or woman, and preacher?
4) Are you mentoring/discipling anyone that is not on your staff?

Spirit-Filled/Spirit-Led Experience
1) How will you support the development and use of spiritual gifts?
2) How do you see the role of and need for the Holy Spirit in our lives?

City Church/Community
1) Our church has been known as a city church. How will you continue that legacy?
2) What do you see as our role in the community and education?

Worship
What do you see as the role of music in worship? What range of styles do you think is appropriate?

Prayer
1) What was the most significant answer to personal prayer you've received?
2) Tell us about your devotional/prayer life. Is this time always spent on your own, or do you ever share it with your spouse/family?

Evangelism
1) What approaches to evangelism do you feel are most effective?
2) Tell us about someone you've recently led to the Lord. (Personally, not from the pulpit.)

Missions
This church has always had an emphasis on the lost and missions. How will you continue that strength?

Personal
Who is your "Paul," and what impact has that person had on your life?

Tithing/Finances
1) How do you encourage the church to tithe?
2) Do you tithe? How often?

Vision
3) What is your criterion for the measurement of success in a church?
4) How do you sense the Lord's leading?
5) It is a given that tolerance is needed, but where must lines be drawn? (Give examples.)

Children
How important is children's ministry to the overall growth and development of the church?

Demonstrated Leadership Questions
Management/Personal
1) What principles do you use to effectively manage your time both at work and at home?

2) How would you, as a pastor, prioritize the many roles that demand your time?

Vision
1) How do you get your current church to see and follow your vision for the church?
2) What recent accomplishments has your current church achieved?
3) Do you regard yourself as a "risk taker"? If yes—respond with examples where risk was combined with your vision.

Change
1) If you felt the Lord urging you to take the church in a new direction or a special emphasis, how would you go about getting the staff and larger church body to follow?
2) In coming to a new church, do you favor evaluating/developing current staff members or bringing in your own people?
3) Give an example of systemic change that you have implemented in a church.

Style
How would you describe your leadership style?

Experience with Staff
1) In the past, how have you worked with leaders under you?
2) What type of relationship do you have with your pastoral staff?
3) What kind of culture have you developed with your current church staff?

Personal

What have you found to be your greatest strengths and weaknesses?

Financial

1) What financial skills do you consider important in pastoring a church?
2) As senior pastor, what do you believe is your proper involvement in financial areas of the church's ministries?

Equipping/Training

1) What do you currently do to equip and mobilize your congregation?
2) How have you developed and equipped your current staff?
3) Describe how you have recruited, developed, and used the body of your current church for positions of leadership.
4) What kind of accountabilities would you put in place for your staff?

Why Our Church

Why are you interested in moving on at this point in your ministry?

Adversity

Describe the toughest time you have had as a spiritual leader and how you came through it.

Church Board

How do you see your role and relationship with the board/governing body?

EVALUATING CANDIDATE APPLICATIONS AND RESUMES

It may be helpful for your team to sort applicants into three categories:

1) "Front-burner" candidates that the search team will definitely pursue.
2) "Back-burner" candidates that the team may pursue later.
3) Candidates that are "off the burner" and will not be considered further.

As soon as you know that a candidate who has contacted you is not being considered, you must promptly send a respectful rejection email.

It's important to remain open to new qualified candidates who emerge or are recommended during the search process. The "Pastoral Transition Survival Guide" warns that many pastoral search teams have members who become invested in one candidate early in the search process. Often, those candidates are not ultimately the right match for the church, and the search team must start over.[30]

DIGGING DEEPER: EVALUATING CANDIDATES' SOCIAL MEDIA AND RECORDS

When you're considering many candidates, you should be able to get by with a cursory investigation of candidates' social media use, including Twitter, Facebook, and online groups.

---

30 Grace Ruiter, "Pastoral Transition Survival Guide."

But once you have identified your top three candidates, it's time to dig deeper. Searching both the pastors' and the spouses' media feeds going back at least one year. Go farther back if you can.

It is also essential to conduct criminal and credit history background checks. Feel free to let candidates know you are subjecting them to such scrutiny. If they try to keep you from doing so, proceed with caution.

PREPARING YOUR NEW PASTOR'S JOB DESCRIPTION AND SALARY PACKAGE

How many Sundays every year do you expect your new pastor to preach? What is your church's policy on vacations and sabbaticals? You need to spell everything out before you start interacting with candidates.

Pastoral candidates will probably ask about these matters. The Transition Leader typically handles these discussions with the final candidate, so be ready to answer the questions, or better yet, provide them proactively:

> Sabbath/sabbaticals offered
> Preaching duties
> Responsibilities with deacons/elders
> Vacation days
> Family expectations, if any, on members of the pastor's family
> Proposed salary package

COMPENSATION CONSIDERATIONS

When it comes to compensation, your team must consider not only the incoming pastor, but also the outgoing pastor and the new pastor's family.

Compensation for Exiting/Transitioning Pastor (and Spouse—If on Staff)

Work with the outgoing pastor (when applicable) to establish the long-term financial ceiling (where should their compensation be at the end of their tenure?) and floor (what is the minimum they need to live on for the rest of their life?).

There are many factors that contribute to these numbers such as if they are founding pastors. Church growth or church assets acquired should also be considered. Most pastors with a planned transition receive a reduced percentage of their package each year until they reach the door.

Compensation for Incoming Pastor

Your search team must coordinate with the church board/leadership and incoming pastor to determine and negotiate his/her compensation package.

Compensation for Incoming Pastor's Spouse—If on Staff

The board should determine and negotiate the pastoral spouse's compensation package if he/she will be working for the church.

CLARIFYING THE FORMER PASTOR'S RELATIONSHIP WITH THE CHURCH

What about the former pastor's relationship to the church? Should he or she continue to a be present, or be involved? After all, it can be very difficult for a pastor who has served a church for 10 or 20 years to let go. That's understandable.

But my experience provides a clear answer. If you want your transition to succeed, and if you want your new pastor to begin shepherding the flock, the departing pastor must stay completely away from the church for at least three to six months. I've seen far too many cases where the outgoing pastor's continued presence and interference created major problems for the new pastor and the church.

This absence should be total. The departing pastor must not come back to the church to conduct weddings, funerals, or other special services. Otherwise, the people will continue to seek counsel from the previous pastor.

The sheep have a new shepherd. The continued presence of the former pastor will only complicate the transition process. It may actually hinder it.

The Transition Leader should put these expectations in writing in a Memorandum of Understanding that is part of the outgoing pastor's exit. The MOU is an essential document that spells out the expectations of both leaders, which can help eliminate misunderstandings.

Using an MOU at the front end of your transition can eliminate confusion and conflict on the back end. I cannot overstate how important it is to have clear lines of understanding as the transition takes place.

I've created a sample memo you can adapt for your use. If the spouse has also been on staff or was deeply involved in aspects of ministry at the church, you may want to create a separate MOU for the spouse as well.

SAMPLE MEMORANDUM OF UNDERSTANDING

You can make your Memorandum of Understanding as short or as long as your situation demands. The following example highlights four major areas of concern.

MEMORANDUM OF UNDERSTANDING

Parties: Departing Pastor John Doe and First Baptist Church of Anytown, Anystate.

Purpose: Defining scope of ministry involvement for departing pastor John Doe and his wife, Joanne Doe, after passing the church's leadership baton to incoming pastor Greg Goforth.

Effective date:

1) Limitations on involvement:

a. Pastor Doe will not communicate directly with any church staff/leadership but will communicate solely through Pastor Goforth, who will manage the relationship and create protocols as needed.

b. Pastor Doe will not serve on the church's official board, though input might be sought in a spiritual advisory capacity by Pastor Goforth.

c. Pastor Doe will have no permanent church office or church office hours.

d. Joanne Doe will have no church portfolio.

e. After the baton is passed, Pastor Doe and Joanne Doe will engage in a sabbatical and be absent from all church activities for a period of three months.

2) Volunteer Ministry Involvement:

Following the three-month sabbatical, any volunteer roles and responsibilities for Pastor Doe and Joanne Doe will be determined by Pastor Goforth. Among the roles and responsibilities considered are:

a. To preach and teach, at Pastor Goforth's discretion.

b. Provide situational mentoring as initiated by Pastor Goforth.

c. Provide leadership training as initiated by Pastor Goforth.

d. Informing Pastor Goforth of requests to perform weddings and funerals for church members.

e. Reserve an available office, conference room, or space when Pastor Doe is hosting a meeting.

3) Time Frame: Indefinite.

4) Gifts:

All gifts bestowed to Pastor Doe by the church or its members are out of good will and appreciation, not tied to current work or promise of future work, and the proper church committees shall oversee the details.

Signed by:

_____ (date) _____
Pastor John Doe
_____ (date) _____
Joanne Doe

WHAT TO LOOK FOR DURING YOUR SET VISIT TO CANDIDATES' CHURCHES

Sure, you want to hear your candidate preach. But you can do that online, and hopefully you did research candidates' sermons before planning your visits to the churches of your top three candidates.

When you visit your candidates' churches, you're examining the whole enchilada, from the way the church welcomes people to the service to how well it picks up trash in the parking lot. Here are the six main things you should look for during your site visits:

1) *Physical Facilities*

How do the facilities look? What is the appearance of things? Does it look like they're committed to excellence here?

2) *Organization*

Check out the ushers, greeters, people who pass the offering basket, and members of the worship team. Does it look like people know what they're doing and why they're doing it?

3) *Assimilation*

As a first-time visitor, you're in an excellent position to evaluate how the church reaches out to folks like yourself. Are they open to receiving new guests? Do they have a plan for church growth?

4) Printed Materials

Do materials you find in the church present the church and its mission in a positive light? How about graphic design? Do the documents you see support the church's identity and mission, or do they seem haphazard and amateurish?

5) The Worship Service

How do you feel about what's happening? Is God there? Do you feel His presence? Does everything flow well? Is the service structured enough, or does it seem so structured that the Spirit is left out?

6) The Sermon

Is the pastor ministering to the church's people? Is what you're experiencing here something that you would like to experience at your own church? Is the ministry of the pastor pastoral, or is the sermon simply a great message with powerful oratory?

CONSULT BEFORE YOU CALL

Your team needs to keep the congregation up-to-date at every stage in the process through announcements at Sunday services and updates via newsletters and the church website.

Communication is even more important as the team prepares to call one candidate. The search committee will take a secret ballot vote to determine the final candidate. Ask the church to pray for the team and the process during this crucial period, and provide them with plenty of time to meet the candidate in personal settings before hearing him or her preach.

YOU'RE ALMOST THERE

If your committee has done its homework, and the congregation has honored and supported the process in prayer, the vote outcome should bring no big surprises.

But hold on. The transition process isn't over quite yet.

Transition in Churches Post-COVID

The COVID-19 pandemic never ended. It still kills hundreds of Americans every day. The pandemic has also left its mark on churches. How has COVID-19 affected your church, and how will this alter your search process?

In January 2021, 29 percent of pastors considered resigning. In March 2022, 42 percent of pastors considered resigning according to research by George Barna. The three biggest reasons—as cited earlier—were "immense stress," feelings of isolation and loneliness, and "political division."[31]

By the end of 2022, it was clear that fewer than 42 percent of pastors resigned, but many said they are just thinking about leaving. Others hope to retire early. But it's not yet clear who will replace all these retiring pastors. Students still attend seminaries, but fewer students are training for pastoral careers. Some congregations have seen job openings go unfilled for extended periods of time.

---

[31] "Pastors Share Top Reasons They've Considered Quitting Ministry in the Past Year," *Barna Group*, 27 Apr. 2022, https://www.barna.com/research/pastors-quitting-ministry/.

Clergy are under intense stress compounded by loneliness brought about by the concern that they can't speak openly about their thoughts or feelings to anyone in these divisive, social-media-driven times.

Many pastors also face a smaller but increasingly angry and divided flock.

Times of Turmoil and Decline

Steve Rabey, in his article "Colorado Springs ministry helps pastors address post-COVID stress, depression"[32] writes:

For decades, more than two-thirds of Americans belonged to a church. But by 2020, less than half were church members, an unprecedented low since Gallup started keeping track in 1937.

Americans' trust in churches and pastors has fallen, too. Gallup reported that in 2009, 52 percent of adults had confidence in the church as an institution. By 2021, only 37 percent did, and only 36 percent had trust in pastors, a new low.

Pastors regularly face stress, and many deal with depression, but COVID sent rates of stress and depression soaring.

Ministering to Ministers

Rabey continues:

Basically, no matter what choice they made, there were going to be lot of people upset," says Giles Armstrong, President of SonScape Retreats, a Colorado ministry that has helped

---

32 Steve Rabey, "Colorado Springs Area Ministry Helps Pastors Address Post-Covid Stress, Depression," *Colorado Springs Gazette*, 14 Aug. 2022, https://gazette.com/life/colorado-springs-area-ministry-helps-pastors-address-post-covid-stress-depression/article_a660ff38-132d-11ed-a755-bf751c8f8fc5.html.

thousands of pastors, missionaries and other Christian leaders with its weeklong retreats since its founding in 1984.

Many pastors tell Armstrong that decisions they made about masks and other issues ignited divisions rivaling the intensity of the "worship wars" that pitted hymn-loving traditionalists against those who favor contemporary worship music.

COVID temporarily prevented many churches from meeting, which led many congregations to scramble and put Sunday services online for the first time.

Decisions about when to resume in-person services caused controversy, and many congregants chose to continue watching services from the comfort of home, or migrated to other online services more to their liking. At many churches, attendance has not returned to pre-COVID numbers. Hundreds of smaller churches have closed, and hundreds of pastors have resigned.

Decisions about whether or not to require face masks led to new divisions, says Armstrong, who worked as a pastor in Berean churches before joining SonScape in 2019.

Some people said, "If we wear masks, I'm not coming." While others said, "If we don't wear masks, I'm not coming." Pastors ran themselves ragged trying to meet the needs of their people in a constantly shifting system that might change in a week or two."

Armstrong says the new pressures COVID put on churches exposed congregations' lack of spiritual vitality and maturity, making things harder for pastors, the leaders Peter called the "shepherds of God's flock."

> "Pastors are trying to figure out how to shepherd sheep that don't love the other sheep," Armstrong said. "And if we can't love the person in the pew next to us, how can we love the person in our community that we're supposed to be reaching for Christ?"
>
> Now, many pastors are struggling with how they can get members to love one another, or at least quit fighting each other.
>
> "In their hearts, shepherds want to serve people and love people," Armstrong says. "To have a lot of people upset with them devastates a pastor's heart."

Politics Ups the Pressure

Rabey also reports:

Partisan politics have increased division in the pews. Pastors are being challenged to use the pulpit for partisan purposes, including candidate endorsements and positions on controversial legislation. Those who don't speak out can be labeled weak or woke.

Armstrong, who has lived in foreign countries, believes America is "one of the greatest nations on Earth." But he fears some churches are too politically entrenched.

"The challenge is: Are we here to save America or save Americans? Are we trying to save a way of life instead of living our lives in such a way that we reveal Jesus, the author of life?"

Declining Rewards

That's not all. Mya Jaradat, in an article for the *Deseret News*, explains:

> While the responsibilities of the pastoral calling have grown more complex, the rewards have decreased. The small, spontaneous and positive interactions with church members that previously kept clergy going—stopping in a hallway to chat with a congregant, a warm smile—disappeared from the work over the past two years.[33]

---

33 Mya Jaradat, "Religious Leaders Struggle with Burnout, Depression and Anxiety - Just like the Rest of America." *Deseret News*, 12 May 2022, https://www.deseret.com/faith/2022/5/11/23058739/religious-leaders-struggle-with-burnout-depression-and-anxiety-pastor-mental-health-worker-shortage.

CHAPTER 13
The Final Lap

Paul encouraged the Corinthians to remain faithful to the end. "Do you not know that in a race all the runners run, but only one gets the prize? Run in such a way as to get the prize" (1 Corinthians 9:24).

A leadership transition doesn't end the moment the congregation votes to accept the new pastor. The race isn't over yet. The prize isn't yet won. The new pastor and the church need to make their marriage work. That's why I insist that the Transition Leader doesn't completely disappear once the new leader is installed but continues to help leadership during the first six months of the new leader's ministry. This is the time for post-transition help and support. It is important to coach the new pastor for six months to make sure the transition works effectively.

I'm usually not present at the church after the new pastor begins, but I help the pastor from behind the scenes, staying engaged as he/she navigates through natural (as well as unwelcome) issues that arise during the beginning of their tenure. I ask about everything. What are the sermons covering? How is the congregation responding? How are meetings with the board and staff going? How is the pastor's family adjusting to the move?

This six-month coaching period is especially important in congregations that have been broken by scandal or poor leadership. But even healthy congregations can benefit from the ongoing coaching.

WELCOMING YOUR NEW PASTOR WITH OPEN ARMS AND HEARTS

The church has a new minister. The installation service is complete. The supervisor is gone. It seems like the process is complete. But, in reality, the pastor and the congregation are just beginning a new phase of the process: the pastoral start-up.

Both churches and pastors often overlook the importance of the pastoral start-up phase. Don't overlook this phase if you want your new pastor to last.

Adjusting to a New Pastor

Once the pastor is installed, the real work begins. The pastor starts to minister with the congregation. The congregation waits to see what's going to happen with this pastor. Before long, a few irritants may arise. Maybe your new pastor isn't doing certain things the way people expected; maybe church members aren't doing some of the tasks the pastor thought they were going to do.

Some adjustment of expectations is bound to take place in any relationship. But when irritants arise between a pastor and a church, it's important to handle them as soon as possible. One way to do this is to participate in a pastoral start-up workshop. These workshops can provide pastors and congregations an opportunity to state clearly and agree to the goals and the expectations the pastor and church members have for each other. Work responsibilities for all parties should be carefully listed, and evaluation should be built in.

Helping the Pastor's Family Transition

Not every pastor has a spouse or a family living with them, but for those that do, moving can be a difficult experience for both the pastor and the pastor's family. The pastor's family may miss their previous church, friends, and neighbors. Kids may be adjusting to a new school. Some of their favorite activities, foods, and stores may not be available in your area. At the same time, your pastor's family will also be forming new friendships, exploring a new area, and developing a relationship with your church.

It is important for your church's members to be particularly alert to the feelings of the pastor's family during this pastoral transition period. The pastor's spouse can be especially susceptible to loneliness. Understanding, care, and love from members of the congregation help make this transition easier.

DOS AND DON'TS FOR SUCCESSFUL TRANSITIONS

Sam Chand, the leadership consultant who heads Expand Consulting, has helped many churches and organizations navigate successful leadership transitions. He believes that the new leader plays a pivotal role in helping everyone adjust to the changes to come. In his book *Planning Your Succession*, Sam provides new leaders with the following list of dos and don'ts.[34]

The Do List: Responsibilities of the Incoming Pastor

1) Honor and celebrate your predecessor.

In many cases, the predecessor who left you an organization to lead is loved and revered. Since people are in the process of shifting their loyalties from that leader to you, it serves you well to honor and celebrate him whenever there is an opportunity.

As you celebrate your predecessor, you make it easier for people to make their transitions.

2) Exercise patience.

Following a founder, a successful entrepreneur, or a much-loved senior pastor is no easy task. It requires self-knowledge and patience, diligence and patience, as well as patience and more patience.

It's important to remember that acceptance can take time. How quickly a successor is accepted varies with the organization. In many cases, acceptance isn't instantaneous upon arrival.

It may help if you can acknowledge the grief and loss associated with the change. Be a realist by acknowledging

---

[34] Samuel R. Chand and Dale C. Bronner, *Planning Your Succession: Preparing for the Future* (Huntley, IL: Mall Publishing, 2008).

what people are feeling. Offering them understanding can only help you.

3) Build relationships with people who have the wisdom to give you advice regarding the organization's past.

Create a counsel of trusted advisors, which is sometimes called a "kitchen cabinet." Realize that you need counsel to help you to make good decisions. Then, connect with the right people. Build good relationships with those who have the experience, the wisdom, the power, and the influence.

4) Take time to understand the shifts within the organization.

You may think you know the organization inside and out, perhaps because you were there while you were being developed for your new role. But even though you were in the boardroom before, you were in another chair. Now that you've moved into the first chair, everyone else is relating to you in a different way. When you moved, they changed too.

Because of this power shift, you have to adjust your understanding of the organization.

5) Be flexible and not overly sensitive.

Some people will insist on being your critics. We encourage you to carefully inspect each criticism for some truth that can help you to grow. There is a shred of truth in everything. If you approach criticism from this standpoint, every critic can actually help you to grow into a better pastor, a better leader, or a better CEO.

The Don't List: Major Mistakes the Incoming Pastor Should Avoid

1) Don't expect things to be the same for you as they were for your predecessor.

If people seem resistant, try not to take it personally. Realize that it's a loyalty issue and that some folks just need more time to adjust to change. You can't expect the same response from people that your predecessor led.

Try thinking of your tenure as a bank account. Any bank account requires deposits. In this case, your stakeholders must make the deposits based on their level of trust in you. Getting that account built up takes time. Your predecessor's years of deposits into the account enabled him or her to get the desired responses. Unfortunately, that account was closed when you became the incumbent; you must now establish your own account. In time, your faithful work will yield similar results.

2) Don't be quick to make changes for which you lack the necessary relational equity.

If you start disassembling everything that preceded you or initiating too many completely new endeavors, it's going to put everyone into a state of shock. People who are in shock aren't going to be too keen on making the necessary deposits into your account.

Sometimes, incoming successors make promises or attempt to cast an organizational vision that's totally unrealistic in an effort to get people behind them. Without a relevant track record with their people, they are going to have a very difficult time.

3) Incoming leaders must realize that all change is a critique of the past.

Even something as seemingly insignificant as painting a wall can be misperceived. In some cases, new leaders begin taking too many drastic actions. Their people find themselves wondering what was wrong with the way things were and why it is necessary to make so many changes.

It's always better to start small. Since change that's imposed is change that's opposed, focus on building relationships at first. It's vital relationships that will provide you with the equity you'll need for successful future efforts. You can make incremental changes, but be sure to balance those endeavors with getting the necessary relational support. Until you do, you may find yourself writing checks that you cannot cash.

4) Don't think that people are going to view you like they viewed you before you came.

Hard as it may be to believe, there are people who may have wanted a different leadership candidate in your spot. Sure, they were courteous and pleasant when they met with you during the selection process, but they may have had other preferences.

Don't rush them; give them time to adjust. Sometimes, they may not have been involved in the entire decision-making process; they may have just received an announcement. You have likely had more time to adjust than they have.

5) Don't try to be your predecessor.

Certainly, you should be respectful toward your predecessor, honoring their accomplishments and their character. If you're following a tremendous leader, one who casts a large shadow, it can cause you to feel compelled to live up to that person's accomplishments or reputation. Resist the pressure to become a carbon copy. Your organization doesn't need another person like your predecessor; they need you.

Dos and Don'ts in Brief

Chand summarized these dos and don'ts in the following acronym. He used the word GROW because he believes every leader should grow continually. The letters provide an easy way to remember many of the important transitions that you'll have to navigate.

Grasp the organizational culture as every organization is different.

Respect and honor your predecessor as well as the local traditions and customs.

Organize your strategic thinking and planning while you learn about the organization.

Work at willingness. Be open to criticism; value it, and seek out the opinions of others.

FINAL FAREWELLS

In some cases, the new pastor and I arrange a final event to celebrate the successful conclusion of the transition process and to signal that it's time for me to move on to my next assignment.

In one case, the church held a farewell Sunday for me, complete with a luncheon, greeting cards and letters, a "celebrity" roast, and a final standing ovation.

One woman, who was the wife of a church board member, raised her hand and spoke.

"Pastor Ron, I want to thank you for bringing joy back to our church."

It was the highest compliment I've ever received.

Alton Garrison, a Christian leader who has been a friend and colleague for 25 years, assessed the situation correctly when he put it like this:

"When a congregation begins to love Ron and wants him to be their new pastor, you know they are now ready for their new leader," Garrison said.

There's much truth in this statement. If members of a congregation have come to know, love and respect me during the time I serve as their Transition Leader, it means they are already moving beyond the past and are looking to their future under a new leader.

At the same time, I leave a part of myself in each of the churches where I have been the Transition Leader.

You can't be an effective Transition Leader unless you're willing to invest yourself fully in the life of the congregation. You have to love people deeply and minister effectively for the church to move beyond their emotional attachment with the leadership of the past hurts. People can tell if you are sincere and real.

Being a Transition Leader isn't a job, it's a calling to invest in the future of Christ's church. It requires you to give all you can give, and to become a cheerleader for the next pastor.

The mission is clear: To do everything you can to ensure the new leader's success.

CONCLUSION
Transitioning Through COVID, Post-COVID, and Beyond

People talk about how divided America is and how people can't agree on anything. But I've seen Christians come together time and time again when they vote to bring in new pastors during times of transition.

Because of the work we've done to prepare congregations for the challenges of transition, all the votes on new pastors have come out at least 90 percent in favor of the new leader. That's a resounding vote that demonstrates how things can go right when people seek the guidance of the Lord and respond to that guidance with a unity of purpose.

My concluding message to you is that your church can smoothly and efficiently transition from one leader to the next if you follow the advice I've provided throughout this book.

FACING THE CHALLENGES OF COVID

Many churches struggled with closures, mask requirements, and other challenges brought about by the global

COVID-19 pandemic. When churches were required to limit attendance or cancel public services, many leaders feared the worst. I experienced my own challenges, navigating pastoral transitions through this period, but like the rest of you, we figured things out step-by-step.

David Crabtree had pastored Calvary Church, a thriving congregation in Greensboro, North Carolina, for thirty-three years. During the COVID-19 crisis, he was asked to join the executive team of the North Carolina District of the Assemblies of God.

I was asked to step in as the Tradition Leader to serve Calvary as we walked through the transition process. At first, I was worried. *How can I lead and serve one thousand people online?* I asked myself.

As you've seen in this book, part of my mission as the Transition Leader is to minister to the congregation, as well as church leadership and staff. For decades, I've relied on kind and loving interpersonal communication to help walk people through the process. But I worried about how this process would go now that we had to rely on digital means to get the message out. How would I—the new guy—establish rapport and trust with people who didn't know me and do it all online?

Thankfully, I had a great team to work with. Church staff helped me figure out what to say and how to say it. Quickly, we evaluated and purchased new cameras and equipment that enabled us to produce great Sunday services and keep children's and youth ministries meeting online as well.

Plus, we plunged headlong into online giving to keep our church funded.

We learned to use these new techniques and technologies during months of isolation. We rejoiced when we could finally resume an on-site presence with approximately 250 people in our services. Suddenly, I found it easier to preach, and our worship team felt better able to minister.

Fearful that isolation might make our church become self-centered and inward-focused during the COVID-19 pandemic, we launched new outreach programs serving the surrounding community. Our congregation responded, and before long, several hundred members were gathering every week to serve our city with food and other compassionate hands-on ministries. Calvary rediscovered what it meant to serve others, and that strengthened the church.

Before we knew it, fifteen months had gone by, and more and more people were returning to in-person services. During that time, our pastoral search committee did its work, finding a great candidate, Jon Catron. The congregation agreed with 98 percent of them voting to call Jon.

COVID-19 complications made the whole process more complex, but the pandemic wasn't able to derail our transition.

DEALING WITH POST-COVID CHALLENGES

Once America got through the worst of the pandemic, people wanted to get "back to normal." But today's new normal is different from yesterday's.

Many people still struggle with long-haul symptoms from the virus. Others deal with depression or other emotional issues resulting from the loss of time with friends, social groups, and even jobs that disappeared during these two-and-a-half difficult years of life.

For churches, many pastors resigned after their levels of stress, frustration, and depression rose during the pandemic. Attitudinally, people seem more impatient and exhibit a lack of trust toward institutions in general and in the leadership of these organizations. Some people feel a lot of cynicism, and this kind of environment means it takes pastors longer to build trust with a congregation.

I was asked to step in and serve as Transition Leader for Cornerstone Church in Nashville, Tennessee, in February 2022 after the previous pastor resigned due to personal issues. This pastor had been in place for three years following a transition to him from his pastor father, but his tenure had been challenging. Some people had fled the church before COVID-19 hit, and more people drifted away after the pandemic closed things down. But many members came back once church fully reopened with some remaining in a seating section in the auditorium.

Because this transition process followed a sudden departure, we had no planning in place, which required us to take things slow and steady. I didn't rush things, believing that a hurried process would only increase uncertainty and anxiety.

In many ways, Cornerstone felt like my toughest transition. The combination of COVID-19 and the pastor's departure was a one-two punch that left church members confused, and the staff was both physically and emotionally weary. But I tried not to let on how difficult the assignment seemed.

I began preaching on Sunday mornings, trying to offer healing from the pains of the past while casting a vision of the future with a new pastor. God was faithful, giving me messages and words of knowledge about what to preach and how to lead. Our worship pastors led our people into the presence of God every Sunday. Soon, we began to see healing come to the church. And the church board and search committee were made up of wonderful leaders who sought God's direction and guidance.

And to make sure Cornerstone didn't grow inward-looking and self-centered, we focused on evangelism and outreach. Over a period of nine months, we saw 265 people make first-time decisions for Christ.

Before I knew it, the church members were united in spirit. People had recovered from the sorrows of the past and were looking forward with anticipation to the future. There was an outpouring of love for me and church staff members who had been giving our all.

Finally, on September 25, 2022, the members of Cornerstone voted to call Jeremy Austill as their new pastor. The vote was 99 percent. Hallelujah!

BUILT ON THE ROCK

Churches face many challenges, and frankly, there are many situations in ministry that are beyond what we are humanly capable of enduring. That's why I'm so glad it's not me and other humans running the show. It's the Holy Spirit who works to build up Christ's body.

As Jesus told Peter, "On this rock I will build my church, and the gates of Hades will not overcome it" (Matthew 16:18).

COVID-19 brought its share of problems, as did the recovery. Tomorrow, churches will face new equally daunting challenges. But God loves His church—even when we sabotage it or lose faith in it.

In good times and bad, the Spirit will empower us to serve His church. I hope my experience in leading dozens of transitions over the past twenty-five years will encourage you when you face your own seemingly insurmountable challenges. God bless you as you serve Christ's body!

About the Author

Ron McManus has served the kingdom of God in a variety of ways. He was a lead pastor for 16 years, growing his congregation from 300 to 3,000. He served as the first president of EQUIP, John Maxwell's ministry to provide resources to churches in 100 countries.

Ron is an advisor and consultant to many churches and denominations and has worked most intensely with the Assemblies of God. He has the gift of leading temporarily, which has allowed him to develop a process to assist churches during the in-between phase of permanent senior pastor, helping them to gain health and positioning them to receive a new lead pastor.

He has served as interim pastor for thirteen churches. He has served as a Transition Leader for twenty-two years, leading twenty congregations through the process of change. Out of the dozens of pastors who assume the lead pastor role after Ron served as transition pastor, all, but one, are still in active service today.

Ron also helped develop and taught Acts 2 Journey, a church health and revitalization program that has been used in 2,000 churches. Acts 2 Journey helps churches assess their strengths and prepare themselves for the challenges and leaders of the future.

Ron also developed the Foundations of Leadership program presented to hundreds of pastors in forty-eight states.

Ron currently leads Legacy Transition Group.

Legacytransitiongroup.com

CPSIA information can be obtained
at www.ICGtesting.com
Printed in the USA
JSHW011737080123
35824JS00004B/15